D0911038

The Secrets of
Successful
Business Letters

About the author

Born in Edgware, Middlesex, longer ago than he now dares to think about, Clive Goodworth was for twenty years a regular officer in the Royal Air Force. In 1968 he joined the Road Transport Industry Training Board as a training adviser where he spent two years before becoming a senior personnel executive with an international oil company. In 1975 he went into teaching and became Senior Lecturer in Management and Professional Studies at the Huntingdonshire College. A few years ago he decided to devote himself to full-time writing. His previous books include *Effective Interviewing For Employment Selection* (1979), *Effective Speaking and Presentation for the Company Executive* (1980), *How to be a Super-Effective Manager* (1984), *How You Can Do More in Less Time* (1984), and *Effective Delegation* (1985). *The Secrets of Successful Business Letters* is his first book for Heinemann. He lives in Bury, Cambridgeshire.

Books in the series

The Secrets of Successful Copywriting　Patrick Quinn
The Secrets of Successful Hiring and Firing　Clive Goodworth
The Secrets of Successful Low-budget Advertising　Patrick Quinn
The Secrets of Successful Sales Management　Tony Adams
The Secrets of Successful Selling　Tony Adams
The Secrets of Successful Speaking and Business Presentations
Gordon Bell

The Secrets of
Successful
Business Letters

Clive Goodworth

Heinemann Professional Publishing

Heinemann Professional Publishing
22 Bedford Square, London WC1B 3HH

LONDON   MELBOURNE   AUCKLAND

First published 1986
First published as a paperback edition 1988

© Clive T. Goodworth 1986

British Library Cataloguing in Publication Data
Goodworth, Clive T.
   The secrets of successful business letters
   I. Commercial correspondence
   I. Title
   808'.066651021   HF5721

ISBN 0434 90684 0 cased
     0434 90698 0 paper

Set in 11/13pt Baskerville by Deltatype, Ellesmere Port
Printed by Billing & Sons Ltd, Worcester

*Dedicated with loving affection to my sister, Jeni,
and my lifelong friend and brother-in-law, John Stewart-Smith*

Contents

Reader, are you in difficulty over a particular piece of writing? If so, forget about this list of contents and fly straight to the **Red Alert Index** on page 199. Look up the appropriate topic – and, hopefully, you will find some help.

CTG

Appendices

1 That wretched moving finger 'aving writ

Let's kick off by considering some facts of management life. First, to be anywhere near effective, we executive pen-pushers need to be proficient in the art of written communication. Second, precious few of us are – which, of course, is one reason why, like it or not, we're so damned *in*effective. . . .

Here's a third and equally indigestible fact to take on board – namely, that a firm's letters are its silent but all-revealing ambassadors. If the mail that plonks in your in-tray is anything like the stuff that lands in mine (and, of course, it is) – well, little wonder that we have such a stinking reputation!

But enough of that, please stand by for a disclaimer. The reader who expects these pages to be crammed with a scholarly and erudite exposition on how to write letters is in for a big disappointment – for the very simple reason that, being neither scholarly nor erudite, I happen to detest such deathly boring tomes. No, me hearty, this book is expressly intended for the hard-working, averagely literate person who, when he or she gets into a flap over a particular writing task, can fly to its **Red Alert Index** for a spot of help.

Hullo and welcome – let's get cracking.

Something on the dreaded Po-Style

'Twas only the other day when postie shoved the following horror into my letter-box – written, dare I say it, by a manager.

> **Dear Sir or Madam**
>
> **We thank you for your esteemed interest in our .... range [*I'll leave their wretched product shrouded in the anonymity it deserves.*] and accordingly have the greatest pleasure in enclosing herewith our brochures which we confidently expect will provide you with all the information you require.**
>
> **On receipt of your valued instructions, we shall have pleasure in arranging for our representative to call on you at your convenience, in order to discuss with you which of our extensive range of models would be best suited to your requirements.**
>
> **Assuring you of our very best attention at all times,**
>
> **We remain,**
>
> **Yours faithfully**
>
>
> **(Wots-it Limited)**

Now, I'm a pretty dedicated believer in Sod's Law, so just in case the million-to-one chance has come up, and you, reader, happen to recognize your own handiwork in that monstrosity – well, that's too bad. Wait until you've simmered down, and then do me a favour, will you? When next seated at your desk, yank open the bottom, right-hand drawer –

and, reaching into the back, drag out the package that's lurking between your 1972 diary and that half-eaten, fossilized cheese sandwich. You'll know it by the label – '*The Practising Manager's Po-Style Writing Kit*'.

I'm fairly confident that your desk does harbour such a nasty, because a *fourth* fact of management existence is that the Po-style kit rules the writing lives of a veritable army of otherwise eminently sensible, with-it men and women – and I'm presuming to guess that you're one of 'em. Anyway, if you'll forgive my pushing the metaphor just a wee bit further, it behoves us to open up the Po-style Kit and, figuratively speaking, find out what it's all about.

Note, first, that our mythical package is blazoned with the legend, 'Made in Victorian England'. This being so, I reckon it's necessary for us to take a very swift peep into history if, indeed, we're to understand why so many of us are tainted with our forbears' addiction to the Po-style.

In those halcyon Victorian days, the rapid development of new printing methods and the spread of literacy enabled folk to read as people in Britain had never read before. Circulating libraries, workers' institutes, railway bookstalls and a burgeoning newspaper-cum-magazine industry helped to satisfy the public appetite – and writers, ever-conscious of the regal age in which they lived, laboured hard to ensure that their work accurately reflected the florid extravagance that reigned supreme in their aspidistra-ridden parlours and drawing-rooms.

Note, also, that in this cast-iron world being built to last, there was another and even bigger change taking place – that headlong development of commerce and industry which, as every schoolboy knows, was subsequently and aptly named the Industrial Revolution. Not surprisingly, its teeming Victorian protagonists realized the extent to which their business success depended on communication – on the public need *and* appetite for the written word. So, founded in the redolently rich phraseology of the age, the Po-style Writing Kit became a necessity – and, like all such rock-solid, brass-bound British traditions, has remained with us ever since.

Lest you doubt this, consider just some of the Victorian Po-style ghosts that continue to lurk in our twentieth-century closet:

> **. . .we respectfully beg to acknowledge receipt of your letter dated. . .**
> **. . .we thank you for your esteemed interest in our. . .**
> **. . .we are in receipt of your letter dated. . .**
> **. . .we take great pleasure in confirming that. . .**
> **. . .we hope we may be entrusted with the favour of. . .**
> **. . .assure you that the matter is receiving our active consideration. . .**
> **. . .in fulfilling your esteemed order. . .**
> **. . .and oblige. . .**
> **. . .enclosed please find. . .**
> **. . .we are despatching under separate cover. . .**
> **. . .for completion by the 14th, inst. . .**
> **. . .assuring you of our desire to be of service. . .**
> **. . .assuring you of our best attention at all times. . .**
> **. . .we remain. . .**

And so on, *ad infinitum*.

If we're honest with ourselves, the survival of the wretched Po-style is virtually guaranteed unless and until managers (and organizations) accept that, in order to write 'formal' letters and what-not, it's quite unnecessary and totally wrong to indulge in the grandiose, oft-ungrammatical and clumsy phraseology of the past. With the possible exception of the lawyer (who, it seems, will always confound us with lofty explanations why it is vital to sacrifice simple English on the altar of verbosity), there is little excuse for the business writer who, although he or she usually *speaks* naturally and well, resorts to a totally different lingo when slapping pen to paper.

So, the very next time you're in the vicinity of London's Victoria and Albert Museum, just pop in and leave your Po-style kit in the foyer – for that is where it belongs.

But what about sheer lack of writing skills?

Y'know, for my sins, I've been concerned with management training of one sort or another for longer than I care to recall – and, over the years, if there's one cry-from-the-heart that I've heard umpteen times from adult students, it's this:

'Clive, d'you mind if I have a quiet word? It's, er – well, I'm a bit worried about all the written stuff you're going to want me to do on this course. . . . Y'see, the truth is, I didn't have much in the way of education – and, er, to be honest, I'm not all that hot when it comes to writing things down. . . . I thought I'd better mention it. . . .'

As a complete aside, such a genuinely worried person often overlooks the fact that an arsenal of accrued wisdom can make up for one hell of a lot on the debit side – but, of course, there's no way that it can redress the balance where poor writing skills are concerned. Donning my mortar-board with a vengeance, I must tell you my stock reply:

'Look, me bucko, you're obviously a manager who is keen on the job, and I think you'd be very annoyed if someone referred to you as a lazy tyke – right? So, why on earth don't you get your finger out where this business of writing's concerned, and trot along to your local college? For goodness sake, stop crying in your beer – and enrol on a suitable evening course! Or, if that doesn't appeal, find out where your nearest Open Learning Centre is situated, and get yourself organized with a unit on "Better Writing" – when you'll be able to do the virtual lot at home, sitting cosily at the dining-room table. . . . If senior citizens can hack such a course, so can you!'

If the cap fits, reader. . . .

Style-wise, a recipe for writing success

There are some ground-rules which, if followed, will certainly help to improve your business writing – but, mark you, only if you have a flicker of fire in the belly and a positive determination to work at it.

Rule 1   When contemplating a letter or what-have-you, think carefully in terms of what 'writing tone' is best suited to the subject matter and the recipient concerned. On the odd occasion (the penning of a final demand for payment, an admonition or reprimand, etc.), it may be necessary to adopt a chilly, impersonal tone – but, at all other times, do try to inject some warmth and friendliness into your writing.

Rule 2   While you've got that hypodermic syringe at the ready, give your writing a second injection – this time, with essence of freshness. Don't be one of those horror-composers who, if you'll forgive the expression, delights in peeing clichés and jargon on every page.

Rule 3   Use words that the poor old reader will understand, and that means studying the intended recipient. Go on, admit it – when did you last give a deal of thought to this vital need?

Rule 4   Always remember that the reader is human – and, being human, will succeed in misinterpreting anything that is capable of misinterpretation. Read and reread those pearly words!

Rule 5 Remember, also, that the recipient will likely indulge his favourite hobby of *reading between the lines* – so give a pile of thought to that which you have left unsaid.

And, if you want a sixth rule, I can recommend nothing better than those sterling lines from the Ruba'iyat of Omar Khayyam:

> The Moving Finger writes; and, having writ,
> Moves on: nor all thy Piety nor Wit
> Shall lure it back to cancel half a Line,
> Nor all thy Tears wash out a Word of it.

Hum, think on't!

How this book works

Just in case you haven't bothered to flick over the pages, what you are now holding is, in essence, a basinful of checklists, 'phrase-banks' and representative samples of various types of business writing, bound together with the odd crumb of text.

The **Red Alert Index** is, if you like, the backbone to the contents. If and when you encounter a writing hiccup, look up the appropriate subject – and, hopefully, you'll find some help. I don't recommend that you slavishly copy any of the samples – but, rather, that you use 'em as mental triggers to aid *your* composition. While on this theme, some of the samples include alternative words and phrases in brackets – and, once again, these are merely intended as triggers for thought.

And the best of writing luck!

2   Smoothing ruffled feelings

Unless you happen to work for a big organization where complaints, whether merited or not, come in so thick and fast that they have to be dealt with by a so-called 'Customer Relations Department', the odds are that many of your days will be blighted by the need to go-it-alone in replying to such moans, groans and blockbusters. Unfortunately, it's not only a vexing chore, but a highly risky one, to boot – as exemplified by the following checklist of tactical dos and don'ts:

Dealing with complaint letters – Checklist   (1)

1   Never allow a complaint to smoulder in the in-tray; get a reply off with the speed of light, even if it's only an interim acknowledgement.

2   Always personalize the reply – the use of formal salutations ('Dear Sir', etc.) can be a sure-fire means of fanning the flames.

3   However rude or unjustified the complaint may be, however outraged you may feel, always thank the writer for bringing it to your attention.

4   While that awful old adage, 'the customer's always right,' is strictly for the birds, never make the fatal

mistake of telling a complainant that he or she is wrong. If it is necessary to refute an allegation, use the more diplomatic 'I fully appreciate your point of view, *but* . . .' approach.

5 Always inject the reply with a healthy dose of sympathy – which, when you think about it, needn't indicate surrender.

6 If the complaint is well-justified, take care to word the apology in fulsome terms, but always with a modicum of dignity. The abject admission will do little for your cause, Uriah.

7 Never allow your *tour de force* to be signed on your behalf by a junior – for this is the hallmark of arrant unconcern.

8 Remember that the length of your reply will provide a cogent indication to the complainant whether or not you are taking his or her grouse seriously. The five-line, tersely worded missive provides an excellent detonator for further wrath.

9 Whatever the temptation, avoid placing the blame for any clanger on a particular person or department – it's your company that's in the wrong, so be loyal to your staff and use the generic term 'we'.

10 While the complaint may be totally unjustified, re-member that it's often an excellent tactic to provide a tit-bit of adjustment or apology. Done carefully, this isn't creeping – it's good business.

Apologies for boobs and clangers

Apology for accounting error – Sample 1   (2)

Dear Mr Higgins

Your Account No. 4434

Thank you for your letter of .... pointing out the error in our statement for............

I confirm that we did, indeed, receive your cheque in full settlement of Invoice No............, and I really must apologize for our serious oversight in failing to credit this payment to your account.

I now enclose a revised statement – and, once again, would like to thank you for bringing this matter to my attention.

Yours sincerely

G T Phineas-Hogg
Accounts Manager

Apology for accounting error – Sample 2   (3)

Dear Mrs Glubb

Your Account No. DF 5545/14

Thank you for your letter of .... about the final demand for payment of this account.

I confirm that we did, indeed, receive your cheque for .... in full settlement of the outstanding

amount — and, plainly, it was a gross oversight on our part to have thus worried you with an unwarranted final demand.

Please accept my apologies for this lamentable error.

Yours sincerely

A Squit
Accounts Manager

Apology for wrongly fulfilled order – Sample 1(4)

Dear Mr Tetchy

Your Order No. 7865

Thank you for your letter of .... detailing the haphazard and totally inefficient manner in which we dealt with this order.

I have arranged for the outstanding items, together with this letter, to be sent to you today by Special Delivery — and I am assured that they should be in your hands by tomorrow afternoon, at the latest.

Please accept my apologies for the inconvenience you have been caused [, *which could not have happened to a more valued customer*].

Yours sincerely

S H Backscratch
Sales Manager

Apology for wrongly fulfilled order – Sample 2(5)

Dear Miss Anthropy

Order No. 654

Thank you for your letter of .... detailing our totally inexcusable error with your order.

The correct item [, *one Herculean Chest Expander, Model 999,*] has been sent to you today by First Class parcel post – and I am arranging for our representative, **Mr Atlas**, to telephone you regarding the collection of the unwanted 3 Kgs of Footballers' Liniment at a time to suit your convenience.

Please accept my apologies for this most foolish mistake.

Yours sincerely

T F L Fortescue-Smythe
Sales Manager

Apology for delay in fulfilling order – Sample (6)

Dear Colonel Blimp

Your order for 3 Star of India Surgical Trusses (Model 34)

Thank you for your letter of .... regarding the lamentable delay in fulfilling your order.

I have today spoken with the importers, Poona

Health Appliances (UK) Ltd, and have been assured
that a further consignment of Star of India Surgical
Trusses is expected to arrive from Hyderabad within
the next seven days. I have stressed the urgency of
your order, and the company has promised to let us
have the required items within twenty-four hours of
their receipt.

Please accept my apologies for the manner in which
you have been so seriously inconvenienced – and my
assurance that I will arrange for priority delivery of
the trusses as soon as they are available.

Yours sincerely

Elias P Bracket
Sales Manager

Apology for inability to supply – Sample   (7)

Dear Mrs Gamp

Order No. 8474

Thank you for your letter regarding our failure to
fulfil this order.

Unfortunately, due to an inexcusable oversight on
our part, you were not advised that Ramsey (Isle of
Man) Tobacco & Snuff Ltd has ceased production of
British Bulldog Shag – and that, as a consequence,
this most excellent tobacco is no longer available.

I do apologize for our laxity on this occasion [– *and,
as a small recompense for the manner in which you
have been treated, would ask you to accept the*

*enclosed package of Hedgerow Rough-Cut Shag with
our compliments. According to many of our more
discerning customers, this fine tobacco is exactly
similar in blend to British Bulldog – and should
provide you with a most satisfying smoke].*

Yours sincerely

I M Grovel
Sales Manager

Apology for faulty goods – Sample 1 (8)

Dear Mr Pitts

**Thank you for your letter of .... regarding the
faulty operation of your newly-purchased Permafrost Deep Freezer.**

**I am very sorry to hear of the difficulties you have
encountered, and have requested our Service Representative to telephone you in order to arrange a
convenient time when he may call and carry out the
necessary adjustments under the maker's
guarantee.**

*[I would like to assure you that the Permafrost range
enjoys a well-earned reputation for overall reliability in service – and I am therefore confident that,
once your freezer has been adjusted, you will have
no further cause for complaint.]*

Yours sincerely

S G Nansen
Branch Manager

Apology for faulty goods – Sample 2 (9)

Dear Miss Thomas

Thank you for your letter of .... regarding the faulty carbon paper supplied in your last order.

I am very sorry for the inconvenience this must have caused, and I enclose three pads of Lampblack Film Carbon in replacement. I should add that I am taking up the matter of your well-justified complaint with Lampblack Ltd – and, in view of their fine reputation for quality control, am sure they will take energetic steps to prevent any possible recurrence of this particular defect.

Once again, my apologies – and my thanks for bringing the matter to our attention.

Yours sincerely

M Hardnut
Sales Manager

Apology for poor service – Sample 1 (10)

Dear Mr Armitage

Thank you for your letter of .... expressing your well-justified annoyance over the manner in which your group outing last Tuesday was so badly marred by the breakdown of our coach.

I much regret that the return journey from Cromer was delayed by the necessity for our driver to obtain roadside assistance – but, for reasons of safety, he

decided not to proceed until the apparent defect in
the braking system of this almost new vehicle had
been rectified. As you are aware, only a minor
adjustment proved necessary and the journey was
resumed after a delay of some fifty-five minutes.

I am, however, very conscious of the fact that the
breakdown occasioned some discomfort to the
elderly members of your party – and, as a measure of
recompense, have arranged for a refund of ten per
cent of the contracted hire charge for the coach to be
credited to your account.

Please accept my apologies – and the hope that this
unfortunate event, our first breakdown in over two
years of highly intensive coach hire operations, will
not unduly affect your much-valued custom.

Yours sincerely

D Turpin
General Manager

Apology for poor service – Sample 2 (11)

Dear Mr Grumbleguts

Thank you for your letter of .... I much regret
the delay in answering your original query, but I
have been away from the office for ten days – and,
due to an inexcusable oversight, your earlier letter
was left to await my return this morning. [*I do
apologize for this carelessness.*]

I [*do apologize and*] now enclose the catalogues you
require, together with a detailed specification in

respect of the **Xylon Model 554 Multi-Copier**. Please do not hesitate to contact me in the event that you have any further queries.

Yours sincerely

G A Klanger
Sales Manager

Apology for poor service – Sample 3 (12)

Dear Mr Wittering

Thank you for your letter of .... regarding your most unfortunate experience at **La Paloma** last Friday evening.

I am deeply concerned that you [*and your guests*] were treated so badly [*rudely*]. Please be assured that I have taken energetic [*all the necessary*] steps to prevent a recurrence of such inexcusable conduct on the part of our staff.

[*As a small recompense for this lamentable breach of courtesy, I should be most pleased if you and your wife would care to dine at La Paloma one evening as our guests – when I am confident that you would find everything to your satisfaction. Perhaps you would kindly telephone me in order that I can book a table on your behalf.*]

Please accept my profound apologies – and my thanks for so promptly bringing this unpleasant matter to my attention.

Yours sincerely

F Primo de Rivera
Manager

Replies to ill-founded complaints

If there is a moral to be borne in mind when answering ill-founded moans, groans and grumbles, it's simply that all such complaints should be *fully* investigated before putting one's rebuttal in the post. To be shot down in flames by a complainant who, angered by the rejection of his or her approach, then proceeds to shove the proof of the pudding up one's left nostril, is disastrous. So, do get the facts right before leaping into print!

Remember, also, that the gleeful feeling of I-told-you-so relief on discovering that a complaint is ill-founded or spurious should not be allowed to influence one's writing. The type of reply in which righteous indignation oozes from every word is little more than a standing invitation for Nemesis to take a hand. The aim must be – firmly, *politely* killee chicken!

Rebuttal of ill-founded complaint – Sample 1 (13)

Dear Mr Mackay

Invoice 5492

Thank you for your letter of .... concerning the apparent overcharge on the above invoice.

I have investigated the matter and now confirm that the amount charged on this invoice (3 copies of 'How to Save Money the Easy Way' at £5.45 each: £16.35) is in fact, correct.

I am sorry I cannot be more helpful. [*Please do not hesitate to contact me in the event that you have any further queries.*]

Yours sincerely

C H MacAlister
Manager

Rebuttal of ill-founded complaint – Sample 2 (14)

Dear Mr Winthrop

Your Wavescanner Portable Radio

I write to tell you that your radio has now been
returned following inspection by the manufacturers
– together with their technical report, which reads
as follows:

'Wavescanner Model PR5 (Ser. No. 437129Y)

**Despite the fact that this radio is a battery-
powered model with no provision for battery-
charging input or other external power source,
it is plain that an attempt has been made to
operate the set by passing a high voltage current
(230–240 volts AC supply?) through the battery
contact studs. This highly dangerous action
resulted in an instantaneous and massive over-
load of the circuitry, with consequent fusing and
destruction of many component parts. The set is
beyond economic repair. The user should be
warned of the major hazards involved in
attempting to connect a high voltage supply to
any battery-operated equipment.'**

As I am sure you will appreciate, the maker's guarantee has been invalidated as a result of the misuse of
this radio, and I much regret that I can be of no
further help. I should be glad if you would kindly
arrange for the collection of the set, or, alternatively, authorize me to dispose of it as scrap.

Yours sincerely

J D Sparks
Manager

Rebuttal of ill-founded complaint – Sample 3 (15)

Dear Mrs Butt

Thank you for your letter of .... expressing your dissatisfaction over the outcome of our Service Representative's visit to your home last week.

While I am indeed sorry that you have been so inconvenienced by the breakdown of your Eureka Twin-Tub Washing Machine, I note that the appliance is now ten years old – and that it has been in regular, twice-weekly use since purchase. With this long period of virtually faultless service in mind, I have checked our Representative's report and am afraid I must confirm his diagnosis that the spinner motor requires replacement.

My personal view is that, given the age of the appliance and the consequent risk of mounting repair bills, it would be wise to consider the purchase of a new machine at this stage. If you do feel so inclined, I should be glad to show you our extensive range of automatic and twin-tub models – and, of course, discuss the important question of which machine would be best suited to your needs.

Please do not hesitate to contact me in the event that I can be of any further assistance.

Yours sincerely

Timothy G Suds
Manager

Outright rejection of complaint – Sample 1   (16)

Dear Mr Winge

Thank you for your letter of ....

I have carefully considered all the additional points you have raised, but much regret that [, *as explained in my earlier letter,*] I can be of no further help in this matter.

Yours sincerely

H R Bristle
General Manager

Outright rejection of complaint – Sample 2   (17)

Dear Mr Splatt

Thank you for your letter of .... regarding . . . [*in relation to your* . . .].

I have now conducted a thorough investigation [*into the events and circumstances which prompted your complaint*] [*of all the relevant facts*] and much regret that I am unable to [*comply with your request*] [*take this matter further*].

Yours sincerely

A B Hardacre
General Manager

3 Pay up – or else . . .

You may agree that the secret of effective debt collecting is the rapid achievement of two, simple objectives:

to prod and, later on, scare the recalcitrant beggars into parting with their cash;
but, with very few exceptions, *not* to so prod, anger or scare 'em to the point where they take their future business elsewhere.

Hum, well, the flamin' trouble is, no one has discovered the magic formula for success – which, let's face it, is one hell of a way to introduce a chapter on 'pay up – or else' letters. However, be that as it may, there are a few rules which I can thoroughly recommend to your attention.

Writing collection letters – Some general rules (18)

1 Use a word processor with a letter-quality printer for the production of all collection letters. The 'individually typed', personalized missive has stacks more impact than the mass-produced variety – however many gimmicks the latter may contain.
2 Be persistent.
3 Couch the initial approaches in firm, albeit friendly terms.

4   Always include a 'cop-out' clause in the first letter; e.g.,
    'If you are not satisfied with the goods supplied to you, we
    ask . . .'.
5   Don't fall into the temptation of adopting a Po-style in
    those earlier letters just because you're dunning for
    money. For example, refrain from sending a formal,
    'Dear Sir' letter to Mr Scrooge, when the informal
    variety is far more likely to get results – 'attaching a
    name' to a debt tends to personalize responsibility for it.

Initial reminders to pay

Initial reminder – Sample 1   (19)

Dear Mr Bottletop

Account No. 4318/34

**We should like to draw your attention to the fact that
your [*company's*] account for £183.56 is still outstanding.**

**If you are satisfied with the goods supplied to you,
we ask that you kindly settle the account as soon as
possible.**

Your sincerely

**J H Phripp
Accounts Manager**

[*Note   Some outfits favour the use of an additional sentence in these early
reminders; namely, 'If you have already posted your cheque to us, please ignore
this letter'. But, think on't. . . . If the debt has been paid, your reminder will
have plonked into the waste paper basket long before the reader's eye gets to this
final sentence – so any such trite request is really a bit of superfluous courtesy.
You can be damned certain he'll ignore it. . . .*]

Initial reminder – Sample 2   (20)

Dear Mr Bottletop

Account No. 54365

According to our records, you have not yet settled your account [*issued your company's cheque*] in respect of goods supplied on .... You will note that the amount outstanding is £74.98.

I trust that the goods were to your [*company's*] satisfaction and would appreciate your kind co-operation in settling this [*achieving settlement of this*] account as soon as possible.

Yours sincerely

J H Phripp
Accounts Manager

Second reminders to pay

As we all know to our cost, there are many occasions when initial reminders to pay produce nothing but a deafening silence from the debtor – and our successive letters must, perforce, reflect a definite hardening of tone. But, like it or not, the 'second' missive should never be a vehicle for armour-piercing, blockbuster phraseology – it would be very silly to thus shoot one's bolt so early in the fray.

Second reminder – Sample 1 (21)

Dear Mr Bottletop

Account No. 4318/34

On ...., I wrote to you concerning your [*company's*] unpaid account amounting to £183.56.

We are concerned to have had no reply from you on this matter and would be grateful to receive a cheque in full settlement of the outstanding sum without further delay.

Yours sincerely

J H Phripp
Accounts Manager

Second reminder – Sample 2 (22)

Dear Mr Bottletop

Account No. 54365

I note that the above account for £74.98 has not been settled.

As I have received no reply to my letter of ...., I must now request that payment be made at the earliest possible date.

Yours sincerely

J H Phripp
Accounts Manager

Second reminder – Sample 3 (23)

There is, of course, another approach – which, for want of a better name, we'll label the transatlantic, 'let me be your pal' tactic. My personal reaction to this type of letter is a profound 'yuk', but it could just be your cup of tea. . . .

Dear Mr Bottletop

Account No. 4318/34

I am sure that unforeseen circumstances must have prevented you from settling your [*your company's*] unpaid account amounting to £183.56.

However, I did write to you on .... asking you to kindly attend to the matter, but you have neither sent us your [*company's*] cheque nor replied to my letter.

I am sure you will appreciate that any further delay in payment can only jeopardize your future arrangements for credit — and, in order to avoid such unpleasantness, I would urge that you clear this outstanding account immediately [*make immediate arrangements to clear this outstanding account*].

Yours sincerely

J H Phripp
Accounts Manager

Third reminders to pay

Whether or not you send a third reminder before resorting to the final broadside is, of course, a matter of policy. In deciding thus, it may be worth bearing in mind that when many debtors get wind of the fact that you send 'x' number of simple reminders before slamming 'em with the threat of legal proceedings, they'll hold off payment until you've gone through the known number of 'pleasantries'. So, when dealing with such folk, a third reminder merely extends their period of credit – and helps them, not you.

Third reminder – Sample   (24)

Dear Sir

Account No. 4318/34

As you will be aware, we have now submitted our statement in connection with the above account on .... occasions, and reminded you twice that the amount of £183.56 was still outstanding.

Clearly, this situation cannot be permitted to continue and we must urge you to let us have your cheque immediately.

Yours faithfully
for Klingers Ltd

Accounts Manager

Final demands for payment

Final demand – Sample 1   (25)

Dear Sir

Account No. 4318/34

As we have received no replies to our letters of ....

we have no option but to inform you that unless we receive a cheque for the sum of £183.56 within seven days we shall place the matter in the hands of our solicitors.

**Yours faithfully
for Klingers Ltd**

Accounts Manager

Final demand – Sample 2 (26)

Dear Sir

Account No. 4318/34

Further to our letters of .... in connection with the above account, we must inform you that we shall have no alternative but to put the matter in the hands of our solicitors if your cheque for £183.56 is not received by 1st ....

**Yours faithfully
for Klingers Ltd**

Accounts Manager

Debt recovery and the dirty tricks department

Before you plough on, reader, let's get one thing straight. . . . If, on perusing the next few bits, you feel inclined to cry, 'But that's unethical . . .,' please do so into your beer – for, rest assured, I'm well aware of the fact. I'm no evangelist and, if

I'm to cater for all tastes – well, for all I know, you might be Old Nick, himself.

It often transpires that deliberate delay in payment is not a matter of *company* policy, but simply reflects the philosophy of the accounts wallah concerned – in that a goodly number of these worthies would rather give blood than pay their firm's bills on time. To such folk, it doesn't matter a tinker's cuss that the cash flow situation is radiant with health – it just *hurts* 'em to part with money. Faced with the probability of this type of situation, a simple and sometimes effective dirty trick is to prepare *two* word-processed, letter-quality copies of the second reminder – and send one of them to the managing director of the company concerned, with the envelope clearly annotated for his personal attention. It may just be that Big Daddy'll blow his top and tell his accounts manager in no uncertain terms to get his finger out.

I know of one wily manager who, when dealing with an artful dodger, will 'mistakenly' enclose a file copy of his second reminder in the envelope to the customer – and, lo, this will bear a pencilled annotation along the lines of, 'To solicitor in seven days' time, JHP, 13/3,' or, 'Close credit facility if not cleared by 20/3. JHP, 13/3.' He tells me it works on nearly every occasion.

When dunning an individual (although it might well work where some firms are concerned), there's always the hoary but oft-effective trick of increasing the amount on the second statement, or within the first reminder, by the odd £150, or so. Such an overcharge is calculated to bring many otherwise slow payers roaring into the fold.

Anyway, over to you.

Chasing suppliers

Since 'deliver – or else' letters are almost kith and kin of the 'pay up' variety, this seems as good a place as any to shove in a few samples – so here goes.

Again, it makes good sense to find out the name of the

manager concerned, and personalize the letters – this really does make many recipients feel subconsciously that they're actually involved in the let-down, and that they must do something about it.

Chasing a supplier – Sample 1 (27)

Dear Mr Gristle

Our Order No. 6382

When the above order was placed with your representative, Mr Proops, we were assured that the goods would be supplied within fourteen days. As there has so far been a delay of over a month, I must ask that you kindly let me know immediately when we may expect delivery.

Yours sincerely

R D Timms
Purchasing Manager

Chasing a supplier – Sample 2 (28)

Dear Mrs Thompson

Our Order No. 2148

It is now more than a month since I wrote requesting replacement of five defective sprocket bars (Part No. 77658/27) supplied as part of the above order.

Unfortunately, this is not the first occasion on which we have had cause to complain about your

firm's apparent reluctance to replace defective goods. I really must insist that you let me know immediately when these urgently required parts will be delivered.

Yours sincerely

**F G Greene
Service Manager**

Chasing a supplier – Sample 3   (29)

Dear Mr Spooner

As you will be aware, there have been many occasions during the past three months when we have had cause to complain about your company's failure to meet 'firm' delivery dates. Unfortunately, and despite your repeated assurances that the situation would be resolved, our orders are still not being delivered on time — with the inevitable consequence that we are now receiving complaints from our own customers.

Clearly, this situation cannot be allowed to continue and, unless your company can ensure that delivery dates are promptly met in future, we shall be forced to take our business elsewhere. It is my hope that such a drastic step will not be necessary — hence this personal approach.

Yours sincerely

**J Lygate
General Manager**

4   On flogging one's wares

Quoting the transparently obvious, if sales blurbs are to be viewed by their target-recipients as anything other than unsolicited, time-wasting rubbish, it's vital that the reader's interest is hooked – and held – right from square one. This being so, you don't need me to remind you of the result – the eye-catching, mind-boggling and oft-dubious letters and packages that, dreamed up by specialist punter-bashers, come whiffling into our in-trays with monotonous regularity. And, of course, it goes without saying that if you happen to employ such esoteric methods in the pursuit of sales, you'll be way above reading this kind of stuff. But, just in case, I'll put it on the line. . . . This chapter is aimed at the legion of hard-working, penny-conscious managers who are forced by circumstances to depend for marketing success on a miniscule advertising budget – and do-it-yourself sales letters.

Having made my point, welcome to the club – let's kick off with another checklist.

Composing sales letters – Checklist   (30)

1 **Courtesy** As with all other correspondence, always maintain a dignified level of courtesy throughout sales letters – which, among other things, means refraining from the beastly temptation to talk down to your prospective customer. For this guy's money, it also

means that the current fad of writing in that heartily-bluff, 'hail, fellow, well met' style is definitely out.

2   **Brevity**   The sales letter composed with 'telegraphic' brevity will most likely end up where it deserves, in the wastepaper basket – along with its opposite number, the pages-long *magnum opus*. When striving to achieve the happy medium in length, remember to fit the paper to the words, and not vice versa – a damned silly little paragraph plonked in the middle of an arid, A4 desert simply begs for trouble. Oh, yes, I know, we've all seen those vast advertisements in the press with an itsy-bitsy slogan stuck in the middle of acres of blank space – but, believe me, it doesn't work in a letter.

3   **Clarity**   Bearing in mind that the average recipient will bend only half an eye (and even less of his or her mind) to the business of reading your sales pitch, ensure that your message is put across in direct and crystal-clear terms. The writer who waffles had better take a quick course in storekeeping – for there's going to be one hell of a lot of goods on the shelves.

4   You should know what's coming next – a personal letter will achieve far more than its 'orrible counterpart, the circular. Make it a golden rule to implement and constantly increase your list of *named* contacts – and remember, also, that a personal letter must be exactly that, and not a jaded, mass-produced mockery of the genuine article.

Follow-up letters to new customers

Never allow (as if you would) the happy advent of a customer's first order to pass by without a prompt sales-pitch acknowledgement – and, on such occasions, forget the cost of postage stamps and send the letter in a nice, posh envelope – *not* enclosed in a brown job along with the invoice. And if, as is so often the case, the signature on this important first order form is well-nigh illegible, then do take the trouble to ring the firm up and ascertain the name of the person concerned. There's no need to bother the individual – a crafty word with the telephonist or a handy secretary is all that's required.

Follow-up sales-pitch to a new customer – Sample 1   (31)

Dear Mr Everard

Your Order No. .... [*order for ....*] has now been actioned and I would like to take this opportunity to thank you for your interest in our company [*our .... range*]. We strive to maintain a close relationship with all our customers, so please do not hesitate to contact me in the event that I can be of further assistance.

It occurs to me that you may not have the latest edition of our full catalogue, and I now enclose a copy of this for your information [, *together with an order form*] [*together with a Priority Order Form – which has been specially introduced to ensure the promptest possible service to our regular customers*].

With all best wishes,

Yours sincerely

Ivor Twitchet
Sales Manager

Follow-up sales-pitch to a new customer – Sample 2 (32)

Dear Mr Murd

Your Order No. ...... [*order for* ....] is very much appreciated, and it is my hope that this will mark the start of a continuing and prospering relationship.

Since we pride ourselves on maintaining the 'personal touch' in dealing with our customers, I would like to think that you will not hesitate to contact me in the event that I can be of any assistance.

[*I enclose a copy of our latest catalogue for your information, together with an order form.*]

With all best wishes,

Yours sincerely

C H Hunsley
Sales Manager

Follow-up sales-pitch to a new customer – Sample 3 (33)

Dear Miss Chortle

Thank you so much for your Order No. ...... [*order for* ....], which has now been actioned.

It occurs to me that you may not have the latest edition of our catalogue, and I am happy to enclose a

**copy for your information – together with price lists
and an order form.**

**If you have any difficulty determining your future
needs, please do not hesitate to contact me.**

Yours sincerely

**V R Wright
Sales Manager**

Sales letters in general

If, say, you happen to be in the business of selling clerical
collars, it's likely that you'll not be over-enthused *or* helped
by my providing sample-letters pushing the sale of ortho-
paedic beds, perfumed stationery, ear-wax solvent or whatever. So, for the purposes of this section, I'm going to take a
different approach. . . .

A pick-and-mix phrasebank for sales letters

Sales letters – opening phrases and what-not (34)

**An economic recession [*expanding yet highly
competitive economy*] never fails to add to the
burdens facing any manager [*business*] [*company*].
Today, most thinking executives are personally
concerned with such problems as. . . .**

**Today, as we prepared to send you the enclosed
catalogue [*brochures*] [*literature*] [*leaflets*]
[*describing our latest . . .*] [*the amazing new . . .*], it
occurred to me that there are some features of our
service which we often fail to point out to our
[*regular*] customers. . . .**

We find it very gratifying that for .... years we have enjoyed the privilege of your [*company's*] custom. Clearly, we wish to do everything possible to enhance such a long-standing relationship – and, to this end, I [*we*] think you should be among the first of our customers to learn of [*benefit from*]. . . .

As one of our most valued customers, I am [*we feel*] sure you will wish to know [*to learn*] that. . . .

In enclosing our latest catalogue for your information, I am sure you would wish me to draw your attention to. . . .

Your valued order was received this morning, and I would like to take this opportunity to thank you for your continued confidence in our products. Clearly, we wish to do everything possible to foster our long-standing relationship – and, to this end, we have decided [*are introducing*]. . . .

In these days of ever-rising costs, it is a pleasure to be able to tell you that. . . .

As one of our most valued [*and regular*] customers, it gives me great pleasure to enclose [*to tell you that*]. . . .

As one of our most valued [*and regular*] customers, I am sure you will agree that our strategy of rigorously pruning prices while, at the same time, ever-improving our product range, has done much to cement our [*long-standing*] business relationship. With this policy of continuous improvement firmly in mind, I now write to tell you about our latest, cost-cutting innovation. . . .

At long last, some good news – and we think that you should be among the first of our regular customers to hear [*share*] it! Despite the spiral of ever-increasing costs [*prices*], we are very pleased to tell you that. . . .

Sales letters – eulogizing the product-cum-service (35)

   . . .the finest of its type manufactured today. . .

   . . .the quality that inspires buying confidence. . .

   . . .for the personal attention you can expect from a family firm. . .

   . . .a first-class job at a first-class price. . .

   . . .today's technology at yesterday's price. . .

   . . .whatever you need – at the price you need. . .

   . . .don't even consider a new . . . . until you call us. . .

   . . .for the finest . . . . deal in town. . .

   . . .experience counts. . .

   . . .when you need a *totally* professional service. . .

   . . .our vast range of . . . . at prices to suit you. . .

   . . .when we say '24 hour emergency service,' we mean it. . .

   . . .a fast, friendly and FULL service. . .

   . . .off-the-shelf service – all day, every day. . .

   . . .for the very best in. . .

   . . .tell us how we can help – we'll do the rest. . .

   . . .you're only a phone call away from. . .

   . . .quality . . . . by the people who care. . .

   . . .we'll wager it costs less than you think. . .

   . . .harness space technology at a down-to-earth price. . .

   . . .see your money go further. . .

   . . .get it right, be sure. . .

   . . .where the best costs less. . .

   . . .cut your costs with. . .

   . . .one of the country's most caring suppliers. . .

   . . .try us – and we'll take care of everything. . .

. . .the ultimate in .... equipment. . .

. . .finding the ideal .... is easy — just ring us. . .

. . .when it comes to personal service, small *is* beautiful. . .

. . .your people are our most valuable asset. . .

. . .it won't print money, but it'll help you make it. . .

. . .you have the plans, we have the means — let's get together. . .

. . .can you *afford* to give us a miss. . .

. . .if you need a *fast* service at a *low* price. . .

. . .if it's needed yesterday, we'll come up trumps. . .

. . .the professionals on your doorstep. . .

. . .if you can't call in, ring in. . .

. . .repairs, replacements — then look no further. . .

. . .why go to the expense of hiring a. . .

. . .for that extra pair of hands. . .

. . .the cost-conscious professional service for ALL your .... needs. . .

. . .our wealth of experience and quality of service are second to none. . .

. . .the friendly and efficient service you've every right to expect. . .

. . .we'd much like to show you our massive range of top quality. . .

. . .there's more to our range than you'd imagine — and all at less than you'd think. . .

. . .we can guarantee that our prices will be highly competitive — and our service tailored exactly to your requirements. . .

. . .specialists in the repair and servicing of all types of. . .

. . .your most competitive .... dealer. . .

. . .it's not often you can use a specialist and actually SAVE money. . .

. . .huge selection of ...., ..., ... and everything you need for the. . .

...the leading .... in your area, with the widest range of .... and all other .... requirements...

...the buck stops here – try us for *all* your .... needs...

...for fine quality .... products to enhance your company's reputation, at astoundingly low prices...

...we've been established for .... years, and we aim to make our future as bright as our past...

...we provide the finest professional service in .... equipment in the area – and invite you to put us to the test...

...we offer the widest choice *and* the best value – why not try to prove us wrong...

...a new kind of service from a new kind of dealer...

...who else offers the free loan of equipment while yours is being repaired...

...take it from us, we're well worth looking at...

...and, last but not least, we will better any displayed price in the area – and that's a promise...

...as manufacturers, exporters and major distributors of...

...we are dealers with a difference...

...you name it, we'll make it...

...is a family firm which has won for itself an enviable reputation in the design and manufacture of...

...we plan, supply, fit and service to give you the ultimate in...

...with our free planning and design service, you're just a phone call away from...

...we invite you to compare the price and quality before you decide...

...quite simply, the finest quality, the finest choice – AND the finest prices...

. . .whatever your budget, we have something in our range of .... equipment to suit you. . .

. . .we are leading specialists in the field of. . .

. . .get tomorrow's .... system *today*. . .

. . .we have been providing a complete .... service to commerce and industry since. . .

. . .problems? The answer is close at hand. . .

. . .quality, reliability and versatility — backed up by a totally efficient and cost-conscious service. . .

. . .we urge you to try us first for competitive prices and fast delivery. . .

. . .our customer service is second to none — we *guarantee* a same-day response. . .

. . .we've come a long way since. . .

. . .all offices are different in their own way, and we at .... pride ourselves on quality and service in the widest possible choice of. . .

. . .when cost is important. . .

. . .we're more than just suppliers. . .

. . .all you require in .... under one roof. . .

. . .we truly are the one-stop company for all your .... needs. . .

. . .our service will please you — and simply amaze your accountant. . .

. . .we supply the best .... available today, and all our staff (including our telephonist, bless her!) pride themselves on their top quality, professional service. . .

. . .it's no idle boast — we offer the finest service in. . .

. . .we know what makes .... tick. . .

. . .our philosophy is simple — what goes up on our shelves must come down in price. . .

. . .a fast and friendly service with 100 per cent customer satisfaction is one thing, an across-the-board 'No Quibble' guarantee is quite another — but we offer both. . .

. . .we pride ourselves on being the A-Team in .... equipment. . .

. . .whatever your .... problem, our trained personnel can solve it. . .

After-sales blurbs

Since, nowadays, so much law is devoted to customer protection of one sort or another, the wise sales executive will at least try to extract some advantage from a fairly hairy situation; namely (and since the legal beagles have already ensured he has everything to lose), he or she'll really go to town on his or her after-sales blurbs. And, sticking like glue to the golden rule that everyone likes to see their name in print, he or she'll also ensure that they're nicely personalized.

After-sales letter – Sample 1   (36)

Dear Mr Micawber

In writing to wish you well with your recently purchased Zonar Station-Seeker Radio, I would also like to remind you that we pride ourselves on offering a first-class after-sales facility to all our customers.

While, under normal operating conditions, your radio is designed to provide years of trouble-free service, please do not hesitate to contact me in the unlikely event that the set develops a fault. Full information on the maker's guarantee and associated service facilities is contained in the brochure which accompanied your radio – but, as I am sure you are aware, these details do not affect your statutory rights as a consumer.

May you have many hours of happy listening!

Yours sincerely

B A Blyter
Manager

After-sales letter – Sample 2   (37)

Dear Mrs Giles

In writing to wish you much happy motoring with your new Beta Centaur XLR, I would also like to remind you that we pride ourselves on maintaining a close after-sales relationship with all our customers.

Your Beta Centaur is designed throughout to meet today's stringent requirements for safe, dependable motoring in a car which is supremely easy to drive and maintain. As I am sure you are aware, Beta vehicles are guaranteed by the manufacturer for a period of two years from the date of first registration without any limitation on mileage against any manufacturing fault or defective material. Full details of the guarantee, which does not affect your statutory rights, are contained in your Owner's Handbook — but please do not hesitate to contact me in the event that you have any queries.

Yours sincerely

I L Leere
Sales Manager

Free press publicity

While any sales manager worth his or her commission-salt is well aware that dangling a decent advertisement order in front of the local press will often produce an offer of accompanying space for a 'free article,' not all of 'em are particularly adept when it comes to writing such stuff. Plainly, it's impossible for me to even contemplate producing sample articles to suit all tastes and circumstances –

so, although one swallow can never make a summer, what follows is a two-part, suggested construction for a 'general feature article' extolling the virtues of a mythical company.

Free publicity article – 'Up-market' sample (38)

Note Substitute suitable insertions for bracketed text.

What is [Azimuth]?

Incorporated in [1920], [Azimuth Limited] is a [wholly British-owned,] [Oxford]-based company which has achieved a remarkable record of growth through its [design and manufacture] of [electronic navigation equipment] for the [UK and European aircraft industries]. Employing over [700] people at its [modern, custom-built factory], [Azimuth] is justifiably proud of the strong social and economic links it has forged with the local community.

What Growth is Planned?

At the time of writing, [Azimuth] is investigating the proposition that the company should extend its [export trading] activities to [the developing countries of the Third World] — and, to this end, [discussions are proceeding apace with the governments of India, Saudi Arabia and the Hashemite Kingdom of Jordan].

If [Azimuth] is to grow as planned, money will be required [both] to support the company's [intensive research and development programme and to secure adequate expansion of its manufacturing facilities]. [Azimuth] is confident that [, due largely to the unprecedented success of its recently introduced Alpha Centauri Navigation System], this money can be [internally generated without recourse to borrowings].

One of the most significant [*technological*] developments in recent years has been in the field of [*satellite navigation equipment*]. While rightly proud of the part the company has played in this innovative and challenging work, [*Azimuth*] is conscious that it faces stern commercial competition — and [, *much encouraged by the honour of receiving the Queen's Award to Industry in 1985 for an outstanding export performance,*] is determined to apply all its [*specialized research and manufacturing*] expertise to the task of achieving and maintaining a commanding position in the world market.

[*Azimuth*] *People*

[*Azimuth's*] manufacturing and trading success is entirely due to the dedicated loyalty of its hardworking employees, and the company recognizes that [*Azimuth People*] are its most important and valuable asset. As a mark of [*Azimuth's*] respect for its employees, the company goes to great lengths to ensure that each [*Azimuth Person*] enjoys a good, progressive standard of life reflecting individual ability, loyal service and the acceptance of responsibility. The excellent [*Azimuth*] [*pension, life assurance, disability and medical schemes*] are cogent expressions of the company's faith in its employees, and aim to improve their quality of life by removing the very real, everyday worries of [*sickness, disability, old age and death by any cause*].

[*Azimuth*] offers many opportunities for career development and, by dint of objective selection and training, will place [*Azimuth People*] in the work most suited to their abilities — and provide the means by which they may improve their performance and advance their careers within the company.

**[*Azimuth*] *Shareholders*

In addition to the efforts of its employees, the growth of [*Azimuth*] has relied greatly upon the capital supplied by the shareholders, and without their future support the company cannot hope to achieve its challenging objectives. [*Azimuth*] is determined to develop its resources and earning power by continuing to make the best use of shareholders' investments, thereby ensuring that they and [*Azimuth People*] shall share in the fruits of success.

Free publicity article – 'Down-market' sample (39)

Note Substitute suitable insertions for bracketed text.

What is [*Azimuth*]?

It was way back in [*1920*] when [*John Foster, a well-known local businessman*], founded [*Azimuth Limited*] and [*immediately shook the sailing fraternity*] by producing [*his now famous range of nautical navigation instruments*] – which, [*much treasured by traditional sailors*], are [*still in use, worldwide*].

But times change, and in [*1970*] this forward-looking, [*Oxford*] company decided to keep pace with the march of technology by switching its resources to the [*design and manufacture of highly sophisticated navigation equipment for the aircraft industry*]. [*Azimuth*] now supplies its wide range of [*electronic 'black boxes'*] to many leading [*British and European aircraft manufacturers*]. It's no exaggeration to say that [*Azimuth*] keeps 'em flying!

Over [*700*] people work for [*Azimuth*] at their [*ultra-modern, custom-built*] headquarters at

[*Squire's Lane*], and the company is justifiably proud of the strong social and economic links it has forged with the local community.

[*Azimuth*] *is Going Places!*

Not content with its undoubted success in [*Europe*], [*Azimuth*] is now looking for fresh fields to conquer — and is currently talking hard and seriously with prospective buyers in [*India, Saudi Arabia and Jordan*]. One of [*Azimuth's*] strengths is their [*world-leading research in, and development of satellite navigation equipment*] — and this [*, coupled with their ability to finance future expansion from internal resources,*] means that the company can rightly expect to meet AND beat whatever challenges the future may have in store.

They're Not Just Employees — they're [AZIMUTH] PEOPLE!

[*Azimuth*] knows full well that its success is entirely due to the loyalty and dedication of its workforce, and the company recognizes that [*Azimuth People*] are its most important and valuable asset. As a mark of [*Azimuth's*] respect for its employees, the company goes to great lengths to maintain [*excellent working conditions and good opportunities for individual advancement — and, as further proof of the pudding, provides pension, insurance and medical schemes which are second to none*].

Let [*Philip Johnson*], [*Azimuth's managing director*], have the final say: 'We're in a tough and highly competitive business; but, thanks to the splendid efforts of everyone who works at [*Azimuth*], we've achieved an enviable position of leadership in the market — and, believe me, we intend to keep it that way!'

5 Flooring 'em with technical know-how

Require the run-of-the-mill, hard-working Jack or Jill Manager to produce this or that piece of 'technical writing' and it's a fair bet that the task will trigger a hefty bout of lip-chewing, much anxious thought, frenetic a'scribbling and tearing up of notes – and, all too often, an end-result which is less than satisfactory. Yet, in commerce and industry there is a recurring need for very many of us to produce technical business correspondence of one sort or another – so, without further ado, it's the aim of this chapter to provide a bit of help in this vexed field of writing.

Let's start with that regular mini-nightmare, the formal report.

Formal reports

Formal (schematic presentation) report-writing – rules   (40)

1 Write simply and succinctly – remembering that, although the temptation to adopt a Po-style may be well-nigh irresistible, *it has to be avoided like the plague.*
2 Take pity on the reader and keep words, sentences and paragraphs as short as possible.
3 Seek to avoid the use of technical jargon unless *absolutely certain* that it will be understood.
4 Since the year dot, it has been the tradition for all formal

reports to be written in impersonal terms, omitting the use of such pronouns as 'I' and 'you'. While the 'house style' of your organization, reader, may dictate that you remain a slave to this custom, it is worth remembering that it's only a tradition – and is, by no means, inviolable. If circumstances permit and you wish to lend force to your report by stating, 'In my view', 'I am convinced', etc., then do so!

5   A formal report should be structured (schematically presented) as follows:

(*a*)   title, circulation list and file reference, if any (*see* Section 41);

(*b*)   table of contents (*see* Section 42);

(*c*)   summary or synopsis (*see* Section 43);

(*d*)   introduction (*see* Section 44);

(*e*)   main body of the report (*see* Section 45);

(*f*)   conclusions (*see* Section 46);

(*g*)   recommendations (*see* Section 47);

(*h*)   appendices (*see* Section 48).

Formal reports – Sample titles, circulation lists & file references   (41)

Note   Preferably, reports of more than a couple of pages in length should sport a *separate* page for these details.

Sample (a)

CRO/7654/11/2

REPORT ON THE SITE INSPECTION AT DARLANE COLLIERY HELD ON 6 MARCH 1986

Circulation List

S R Black   – Ch Eng (R & D)
M E Pomeroy   – Eng 2 (Area HQ)
T D Smith   – Project Mgr

c.c. G H Hall – PRO

Sample (b)

Ref: RHQ/43173/32

Working Paper No 3
Grippit Publicity Project

Report of the Sub-Committee under the
Chairmanship of Mr F D Griffiths

Circulation

Mr H L Williams – Chairman, P & R Committee
Mrs J D Grove   – Member, P & R Committee
Mr A F Hirst   –   – do –
Mr L G Tench   –   – do –
Mrs G A Young   –   – do –

Copy to: Miss P Sims – Sec'y, P & R Committee

Sample (c)

SECRET

SC/1723/12/3/Pol

PRELIMINARY REPORT ON VANGUARD
LIVE FIRING EXERCISE CARRIED OUT AT
LENTHORPE HEAD ON 14 MAY 1986

Circulation

Air Cdre G D Blackthorne – Air Arm 1 MOD(Air)
Prof L B Hinney – Vanguard Project Leader
Mr F C Leverington – Mgr, Spec Prod'n
Mr C H Marshall – Mgr, R & D Section

c.c Sir Dennis Newborne – MD

Formal reports – Sample tables of contents   (42)

Sample (a)

CONTENTS

	Page
Summary of report	2
Introduction & terms of reference	3
Report of investigation	4
Conclusions	13
Recommendations	14

Sample (b)

Note   This sample depicts a section of the contents pages of a lengthy report – and, hence, provides the reader with greater detail for ease of reference than would otherwise be the case.

CHAPTER 2 – DESCRIPTION OF PROTOTYPE MODEL X22

	Para.	Page
Engine	51	14
Cooling system	54	15
Fuel system & carburation	57	16
Ignition system	61	18
Gearbox & clutch	65	20
Driveshafts & universal joints	68	22
Differential unit	73	25
Braking system	77	27
Electrical system	81	30
Suspension & steering	89	34
Bodywork & subframes	98	37

Formal reports – Sample summary (synopsis) (43)

Note   The purpose of the summary or synopsis is obvious – it saves many readers the chore of ploughing through the entire document when they have no wish or need to do so. If you wish to be loved by Big Daddy (or anyone else, for that matter), always include a summary.

1 SUMMARY

1.1 Construction of Prototype Model X22 was completed on 21 March 1986 and preliminary road trials were commenced on 24 March 1986 at the company's test circuit. The trials proceeded satisfactorily until the morning of 28 March, when Mr Hunt, a member of the trials team, lost control of X22 during high speed braking tests. While the driver sustained only minor injuries to face and neck during the ensuing accident, the vehicle was badly damaged and is considered to be beyond economic repair. The report concludes that the mishap was caused by a serious error of judgement on the driver's part and that there were no mechanical defects or other contributory factors involved. The report recommends that Mr Hunt should be removed from test-driving duties forthwith, but that no further disciplinary action should be contemplated.

Formal reports – Sample introduction (44)

Note   The primary purpose of the introduction is to supply the reader with any necessary background information. It should include:

(*a*)   the terms of reference, typically:
    (*i*)   to investigate and describe a particular situation;
    (*ii*)   to comment on, and evaluate the situation;
    (*iii*)   to draw conclusions;
    (*iv*)   to make recommendations;

(*b*)   confirmation that the terms of reference have been fulfilled. If this is not the case, the introduction will include the reasons why – and, if the terms of reference have been exceeded, due justification must be provided;

(c)   normally, a brief description of the methods, procedures and processes used in carrying out the investigation.

2   INTRODUCTION

2.1   *Terms of Reference.* The objects of this report are to:

    (a)   investigate the circumstances of the accident on 28 March 1986 involving Prototype Model X22, while being driven by Mr P H Hunt during high speed braking trials at the company's test circuit;

    (b)   determine the cause(s) of the accident and allocate responsibility, if any;

    (c)   make recommendations, accordingly.

2.2   The objects of the report have been achieved. Mr Hunt and all other eye-witnesses to the accident have been interviewed, the accident site and wreckage of X22 have been examined, and conclusions drawn. Appropriate recommendations have been made as required.

Formal reports – notes on construction of main body   (45)

1   Bearing in mind that the text of any formal report should be succinct and concise, it is also wise to remember that it should be written in a style which is appropriate both to the reader and to the subject. This does *not* constitute a licence for the die-hard civil servant-type to wallow in Whitehall gobbledegook. . . . Since the main body is the vital meat in the report-sandwich – well, enough said.

2   He or she who attempts to write a report without first compiling a draft is really bucking for trouble. At the draft stage, the writer should aim at presenting the material in a

logical sequence, and check for the almost inevitable omissions and irrelevancies.

3   Having completed the draft, the writer should then edit the thing; keeping a stern look-out for ambiguities and errors in grammar and/or data – and, of course, rewriting where necessary.

4   Having completed the role of editor, the writer should then subject the work to a meticulous examination in terms of its overall readability and consistency.

Formal reports – Sample conclusions   (46)

Plainly, these are the logical inferences derived from the facts set out in the main body of the report.

Sample (a)

12   CONCLUSIONS
12.1   *Mechanical state of Model X22 prior to the accident* Detailed examination of the wrecked vehicle revealed no pre-existing mechanical or other defects which either contributed to, or caused the accident.
12.2   *Cause of accident* On the basis of the specialist eye-witness reports, and contrary to the information volunteered by Mr Hunt, the accident was caused by a serious error of judgement on the part of this driver.

Sample (b)

VII   Conclusions
A   *Mechanical state of Model X22 prior to the accident* Detailed examination of the wrecked vehicle revealed no pre-existing mechanical or other defects which either contributed to, or caused the accident.

B   *Cause of accident* On the basis of the specialist eye-witness reports, and contrary to the inform- ation volunteered by Mr Hunt, the accident was caused by a serious error of judgement on the part of this driver.

Formal reports – Sample recommendations   (47)

Sample (a)

13   RECOMMENDATIONS
13.1   Mr P H Hunt to be removed from his secondary duties as a test driver and returned to his full- time post.
13.2   No further disciplinary action to be taken against Mr Hunt.

Sample (b)

VIII   Recommendations
A   Mr P H Hunt to be removed from his secondary duties as a test driver and returned to his full- time post.
B   No further disciplinary action to be taken against Mr Hunt.

Formal reports – notes on appendices   (48)

While, in essence, appendices comprise material which is supplementary to that contained in the main body of the report, it is necessary to use care when deciding 'what goes where'. Two useful guidelines are:
(*a*)   any lengthy information to which only brief reference is made should normally be presented as an appendix;
(*b*)   any lengthy or complex information to which a number of references are made should be presented as an

appendix, thereby avoiding repetition within the main body of the report.

In cases where it is necessary to support items of information in the report with calculations, statistics (etc.), it will help the reader if these essential, 'background' details are included as appendices.

Informal reports

The term 'informal report' is a trifle misleading, since it can cover a multitude of sins – so we'd better start by establishing some criteria.

Informal reports – notes on format (49)

1 It is generally accepted that an informal report is set out in memo form (*see* Section 50).
2 A main heading or title should be provided (*see* Section 51).
3 Appropriate headings and sub-headings should be utilized to highlight the various 'sections' of the report (*see* Section 51).
4 If required, the report should conclude with the recommended solution (*see* Section 51).
5 Appendices should be used where necessary (*see* the notes in Section 48, which also apply to informal reports).

Internal memoranda – Heading samples (50)

Sample (a)

INTERNAL MEMORANDUM	
To: **Pers Mgr**	Date: **12 Jun 86**
From: **Sales Mgr**	Ref: **CH/342/15/8**

Sample (b)

<u>CONFIDENTIAL</u>   12 Jun 86

To: G Tumbler   CH/342/15/8
        Pers Mgr

From: L Grabbem
        Sales Mgr

c.c.   I Fiddle
       Asst Sales Mgr

Informal reports – Sample   (51)

INTERNAL MEMORANDUM

To: **MD**	Date: **15 May 86**
From: **Pers Mgr**	Ref: **PERS/48/3/86**

PROPOSED PURCHASE OF A MICROCOMPUTER
FOR PERSONNEL RECORDS

1 Your memo MD/26/3 of 7 May 86 refers. The representative from CDA proved very useful, and I can now report on
the viability of the proposal to purchase a CDA microcompu-
ter for personnel records.

Hardware

2 The M545 computer has a bigger memory (128K) than
the M500 (the model demonstrated to us last month) and,
unlike the M500, is a 'package offer' – in that the purchase
price of £790 (plus VAT) includes a colour monitor,
disc-drive, dot-matrix printer and word processor software.
I have read two consumer reports on the M545, and the
computer was rated as a 'Best Buy' in both cases.

Software

3 The representative demonstrated CDA's Perscan software, and I consider this 'off-the-shelf' program to be
ideally suited to our modest needs. In fact, it will enable us
to store and make far wider use of personnel data than I had
originally envisaged.

Operation

4 **Sally Williams, our records clerk, and I found the M545 Manual very simple to understand – and, within the space of an hour or so, discovered to our surprise that we had both achieved a fair proficiency in the basic operation of the equipment.**

5 **I therefore recommend purchase of the CDA M545 package and Perscan software.**

FGH
Pers Mgr

Specifications

In the steamy jungle of technical writing, it is somewhat difficult to pin down a general definition of a specification – for the simple reason that it has become an everyday descriptive term for quite a wide variety of documents. If one sticks to the rule-book (and, of course, we don't), a specification is essentially a statement of specific requirements to meet a given need, for example:

(*a*) a manufacturer of vacuum cleaners has, say, a back-room visionary, whose job it is to dream up new and fortune-earning models. One bright day, our hero comes up with the idea that every housewife in the land is waiting with bated breath for what he terms a 'Total System' – a revolutionary all-in-one cleaner of everything. So, hey presto, he draws up a *prototype specification*;

(*b*) the firm's market research people carry out an investigation of likely consumer needs – and enlarge on the initial vision by producing a *user specification*;

(*c*) having had the idea approved in principle, it is then the turn of the manufacturer's technical design team to produce an *engineering specification* for the projected wonder-appliance;

(*d*) once a few models have been slapped together, they

have to be tested through and through – and, to this end, a *trials specification* will be produced; and so on.

But, as you're well aware, the term 'specification' is also applied to the bits and pieces of technical information that manufacturers deign to include within the manual, or whatever, which accompanies their finished product – and this is where the rule-book is cast aside. Such specifications are very far from being statements of specific requirements to meet given needs; they're merely sets of facts and figures (often very meagre) on performance and design – and it's up to the poor old buyer to determine what his or her needs are, and whether this type of so-called specification satisfies 'em.

To further complicate matters, there are such things as 'general specifications' – which, being merely guides to bigger and better specifications, can cover a multitude of sins.

Specification of requirements – Sample   (52)

R&D/23/2/86

CONFIDENTIAL

CDA COMPUTERS LTD

PROTOTYPE MODEL X34
SPECIFICATION OF REQUIREMENTS

1 Introduction
  1.1 Prototype Model X34 reflects the company's decision to achieve market penetration in the field of low-priced, user-friendly text-editing equipment.

2 Function
  2.1 When used in conjunction with the CDA Electronic Typewriter or other suitably

interfaced equipment, which will double as operating keyboard and printer, the X34 is required to provide an eminently user-friendly text editing facility. The X34 will be a screen-based system with limited document, phrase and format memories, and is intended to offer a fully comprehensive range of text editing activities by means of simple menu instruction.

2.2 The system is required to offer subsequent optional connection to a conventional audio-cassette recorder, to enable single documents or selected memory contents to be stored on a conventional music cassette.

3 Components

3.1 The X34 is required to comprise:

(a) a central processing unit containing an integrated 32K universal memory with an available capacity of 29,600 characters, extendable by 2 × 16,400 characters, thereby providing a maximum capacity of 62,400 characters of available memory;

(b) a typewriter interface;

(c) a display screen with 58 lines, each line with 80 characters, in black on white background.

4 Additional requirements

4.1 CPU To be microprocessor-controlled, with a three-month data retention capability. The CPU is required to be housed in a flat container capable of use as a mounting base for the screen unit, and is to be provided with a suitable turntable for this purpose.
Maximum permissible dimensions: 80 mm (height) × 400 mm (width) × 280 mm (depth).
Maximum permissible weight: 2.5 kg.
Power supply: 220—240 volts, 50—60 Hz.

4.2   <u>Screen</u>   To be rectangular to suit required
lineage, and of minimum height commen-
surate with the design. The screen base to be
provided with a connecting plate designed to
mate with the turntable on the CPU.
Other maximum permissible dimensions:
380 mm (width) × 340 mm (depth).
Maximum permissible weight: 7 kg.
Power supply: 220—240 volts, 50—60 Hz.

5   Reference

5.1   For materials specifications and basic construction criteria, refer to CDA Project
Specification R&D/26/2/85 dated 9 July 1985.

C R Roberts
R & D Mgr   19 April 1986

Detailed specification of requirements – Sample extract   (53)

112   Frames and beams

112.1   Frames and beams are to be of channel
section. The spacing of frames in peak
tanks and the stern should not exceed 0.6
m, and from the collision bulkhead to 0.2 L
from forward it should not exceed 0.69 m.
Spacing elsewhere should be 0.84 m.

112.2   Frames are to be constructed longi-
tudinally, except where converging lines
make this impracticable. Lengths may be
joined (see Drawing 18542/34/87B), or by
lapping the frames.

112.3   Beam knees are to be fitted between
frames and beams. The depth of each knee

should be 2.5 times the depth of each beam to which it is connected.

113 Bulkheads

113.1   A collision bulkhead is to be provided not less than 0.5 L or more than 0.75 L abaft the stem.

Product specification for customer – Sample 1 (54)

THE HORSLEY ARTURA
SPECIFICATIONS

Engine		Capacities	
Bore (mm)	84	Engine sump	5 litres
Stroke (mm)	89	Cooling system	6.5 litres
Capacity (cm³)	1910	Gearbox	1.6 litres
Compression ratio	24 to 1	Fuel tank	45.5 litres

Fuel: Diesel fuel ONLY

Fuel injection equipment	Kompur-Diesel
Fuel filter	Carbgard DV34
Battery	12V – 325 A/64 Ah

Fuel consumption, published in accordance with the standard conditions defined in the Ministry Circular of 7 March 1975:

Litres per 100 km at a steady speed of 90 km/h	4.7
Litres per 100 km at a steady speed of 120 km/h	6.6
Litres per 100 km, urban cycle	6.4

Loads

Kerb weight	Gross vehicle weight	Gross weight with braked trailer 800 kg
1040 kg (2293 lb)	1440 kg (3175 lb)	2240 kg (4939 lb)

Product specification for customer – Sample 2   (55)

TURBO-ACE AUTOMATIC DRYER
Model 5423

SPECIFICATIONS

		Dimensions	
Motor	250 watts		
Voltage	240V 50Hz	Width	24″ (610 mm)
Heater	2000 watts	Depth	22¼″ (565 mm)
Fuse	13 amps	Height	33½″ (850 mm)
Capacity	10 lbs (4.5 kg)	Weight	100 lbs (45.4 kg)

Quotations

Quotations – Skeleton   (56)

Quotation reference number.

Date.

Accurate description of the goods or service.

Price of goods per unit and, if required, per given quantity; or fee/charge for the service.

Delivery dates or any dates applicable to the quoted service.

Terms and conditions of payment.

Carriage charges.

If desired, insertion of the initials 'E & O E' (errors and omissions excepted).

Quotation – Sample 1 (57)

ULTRA-MOD KITCHEN FITTINGS LTD
13 Church Place, Ramsey, Huntingdon,
Cambs PE17 3FD
(Tel: Ramsey [0487] 436231)

Our ref: **QUO/34/86**

G Staunch Esq   **13 May 1986**
13 Cleveland Way
Ramsey
Huntingdon
Cambs PE17 2BQ

QUOTATION

For supplying and wiring one Cakeburn De Luxe Electric Cooker Model K455 to existing power point:

	£
Cakeburn Electric Cooker De Luxe	**376.00**
Plus VAT	**56.40**
	£432.40

(Delivery and connection – no charge)

Terms: Strictly nett, 30 days from date of invoice

VAT No 999 9865 765   E & O E

Quotation – Sample 2 (58)

D J Chatwell
Belmont House
27 Upton Crescent
Sawtry
Huntingdon
Cambs PE18 1QF
(Tel: Ramsey [0487] 251865)

Your ref: **PHS/LB**   My ref: **DJC/4/13**

P H Simmonds Esq   3 June 1986
Training Manager
Stampit Engineering Ltd
Gasworks Lane
Luton
Beds LU1 3QQ

Dear Mr Simmonds

Thank you for your letter of 30 May 1986. I should be glad to conduct the one-day management seminar on Staff Appraisal at your company on 27 June, and I enclose my proposed programme for your consideration.

My fee for this service would be as follows:

For conducting the seminar (maximum twelve participants) and supplying all necessary handouts and other course material (VAT not payable):   £300.00

(Terms strictly nett)

I look forward to hearing from you.

Yours sincerely

David Chatwell

Written procedures and policies

The single, biggest trouble with so many written procedures and policies is that no one can understand them – and, mark you, that often includes the authors themselves. For the manager who experiences difficulty in this rather thorny field of writing, there are some general guidelines which should be of help – so let's start off by taking a crafty look at 'em.

Written procedures and policies – Guidelines (59)

1   Commence by defining the procedure or policy.
2   Describe its purpose(s) or objective(s).

3   Detail the procedure or policy, taking care to 'section-alize' the various stages, steps, etc. – making full use of numbered paragraphs, headings and sub-headings to highlight the sections.

4   Remember to 'link' each stage or step in such a way that the reader will have no difficulty in following the intended sequence.

5   Remember, also, to explain *why* all but the most simple of operations or steps are necessary.

6   Explain the result(s), in terms of whether or not, and to what degree the purpose(s) or objective(s) have been achieved – or will be achieved by following the procedure described.

Written explanation of procedure – Sample 1 (60)

Transposition Cipher

1   The transposition cipher is a simple form of cipher which may be used in emergency when no other code or cipher is available.

Basis of operation
2   In this cipher, the letters of the original text are not changed, but their order is altered according to a key obtained from a keyword. The keyword may consist of one or more words, should contain from eight to eighteen letters, and should be easy to remember and spell.

3   The security of the transposition cipher depends on the keyword, and this should be kept secret. For the same reason, keywords should be changed frequently.

Ciphering procedure
4   To explain the ciphering procedure, the following

example is worked out with a keyword <u>COLLY-WOBBLES</u>:

(a) from this keyword the transposition is obtained as follows:

   (i) the first letter of the alphabet to occur is 'B'; there are two 'Bs'; the figure '1' is written under the first 'B' to occur reading from left to right, and the figure '2' under the second 'B';

   (ii) the next letter of the alphabet to occur is 'C'; under this the figure '3' is written;

   (iii) the next letter is 'E'; under this the figure '4' is written;

   (iv) the next letter is 'L'; there are three 'Ls'; the figure '5' is written under the first 'L' to occur reading from left to right, the figure '6' under the second 'L', and so on until all the letters of the keyword have been numbered according to their position in the alphabet.

The transposition key obtained from COLLY-WOBBLES would therefore be:

```
C  O  L  L  Y  W  O  B  B  L  E  S
3  8  5  6 12 11  9  1  2  7  4 10
```

(b) the message is written under this key, figures and punctuations being spelled out in full. The sample message to be enciphered is '*Cover blown, am returning via safe route. Await my arrival.*' This is written under the key as follows:

```
3  8  5  6 12 11  9  1  2  7  4 10
C  O  V  E  R  B  L  O  W  N  C  O
M  M  A  A  M  R  E  T  U  R  N  I
N  G  V  I  A  S  A  F  E  R  O  U
T  E  S  T  O  P  A  W  A  I  T  M
Y  A  R  R  I  V  A  L  M  E  S  S
A  G  E  E  N  D  S
```

The last line of letters should never be a complete line; if necessary, dummy letters should be added after '*Message ends*' to make the line incomplete;

(c)   the message is now transposed by reading the letters in columns, the order in which they are read being indicated by the figures of the transposition key. The cipher message will therefore begin with OTFWL, which are the letters under the figure '1', followed by the letters WUEAM under the figure '2', and so on;

(d)   the message is written in groups of *five* letters.

(e)   the above message enciphered ready for despatch will therefore be:

OTFWL / WUEAM / CMNTY / ACNOT /
SVAVS / REEAI / TRENR / RIEOM / GEAGL /
EAAAS / OIUMS / BRSPV / DRMAO / IN

If the last cipher group contains less than five digits, *never* complete it to make a five-letter group.

Security limitations

5   This transposition cipher is extremely basic and, given the right expertise, can be broken with minimal difficulty. It is only to be used as a last resort, and *never* for the transmission of classified field report information.

Written explanation of procedure – Sample 2 (61)

(*The text of a company circular addressed to all employees and enclosed with their pay advice slips.*)

FREE MEDICAL COVER FOR YOU AND YOUR FAMILY

Problems. . .

We think you'll agree that there's nothing so important as good health, and nothing quite so worrying – particularly if you're a family man – as a nagging ailment or the thought of a possible illness. For instance, you may have been told that wee Johnny needs his tonsils out, but that nothing can be done until he's worked his way up the very long waiting list. Of course, it could be you, or your wife, who needs some kind of treatment – but, again, the queue is long. On the other hand, it may be that everything is fine – but for how long? What about the totally unexpected illness – or, perish the thought, the sudden accident?

And problems solved!

To ease all these worries, the company is offering free membership of a first-class Private Medical Scheme to all entitled employees. Firstly, let's spell out exactly to whom this new entitlement applies:

The great majority of you are already entitled to membership. Those of you who have only recently joined the company will be similarly entitled once you have completed twelve months' continuous service.

* If you are single – free membership for yourself.
* If you are a married man – free membership for yourself, your wife and all dependent children.
* If you are a married woman, but not the 'sole bread-winner' in your family – free membership for yourself.
* If you have wholly dependent children – free membership for yourself and your children.

How to join the scheme

You will shortly be asked to complete a simple form, giving details of your dependants, etc., and this will automatically entitle you to the wide range of medical benefits available under the scheme – all of which will be explained to you. Briefly, the scheme will pay for all hospital costs as a private patient, consultants' fees and so on, up to a high annual maximum.

So, do think about joining. . . . In future, you and yours can be fully covered against medical contingencies, and on a private patient basis – <u>at absolutely no cost to you.</u>

Written statement of health and safety at work policy – Sample extract (62)

Note There is a duty on all UK employers of five or more people to publish written statements of their general policy for the health and safety of their employees. The following extract is from one such policy.

<u>Branch Managers</u>
14 It is the responsibility of all branch managers to:
  (a) carry out the duties laid down by the Territorial Director in accordance with the requirements of the Health and Safety Policy;
  (b) ensure that all branch personnel are fully aware of their obligations under the Health and Safety at Work etc. Act 1974, and that they are informed of any further legislative or other requirements;
  (c) investigate and report all accidents which occur within their area of authority;
  (d) investigate, take appropriate corrective action and report on any hazards to health and safety, actual or potential, which may come to their notice;
  (e) liaise with the Territorial Training Officer to promote safety training; including first aid, fire fighting, and the correct use of vehicles, machinery and equipment;
  (f) implement all requirements for the training in health and safety of all new and inexperienced employees;

(g) hold regular meetings with all branch personnel to discuss the implementation and effects of the Health and Safety Policy, and health and safety in general;

(h) maintain the Accident Book and any other health and safety records required;

(i) ensure that all branch vehicles, machinery and equipment are maintained in a safe and fully serviceable condition;

(j) ensure that first aid equipment is maintained in accordance with regulations, and that the location of this equipment, together with the name(s) of trained first-aider(s), is made known to all branch employees;

(k) seek to ensure that all protective clothing and other safety equipment issued by the company is used as instructed.

6 Yer writes peanuts, yer gets monkeys

One very good way for a company to lose money hand over fist, heave mud on it's own reputation and, last but not least, bruise the lives of umpteen innocent people, is to make a pig's ear of it's recruitment-cum-selection procedures. A truism, maybe – but you and I know that far too few employers and, hence, *far too few managers* make any real effort to guarantee that their system is:

* *fair* – ensuring that each and every applicant or casual inquiry is treated courteously, fairly and honestly;
* *effective* – in that it produces the best possible candidates for employment;
* *efficient* – in that it is a highly cost-effective method of obtaining those best possible people.

Any Jack or Jill Executive who wishes to achieve these three-fold objectives of fair play, effectiveness and efficiency in recruitment and selection will realize that the quality of the paperwork involved is of paramount importance – and that, me bucko, is what this chapter is all about.

The job description

This formal document states the purpose, duties and relationships of a job – and, apart from its importance in the areas of job evaluation and training, it is a vital prerequisite in recruitment and selection. In short, the manager who thinks it's possible to set about filling any vacancy without using a job description is either a fool or a knave – and you'd better believe it. . . .

Job description – Skeleton　(63)

Identification　The job title, grade, department concerned.

Reporting to　Expressed by job title, not name.

Purpose of the job　An introductory statement of the major objectives of the job.

Duties　A list of the duties involved in the job.

Responsibilities　A statement setting out the job-holder's responsibilities for personnel, money and equipment.

Relationships　A statement of the relationships involved in the job, both inside and outside the organization, expressed in terms of job titles.

Physical conditions　Details of the location of the job within the section or department, normal hours of work, any special or adverse working conditions.

Organization details　Details of the work group the job-holder will be concerned with, position of the job within the section/department/organization.

Remuneration and other benefits　A statement of the pay for the job, together with details of any fringe benefits.

Job description – Sample　(64)

INDUSTRIAL SLIME RECOVERY LTD
Job Description
Job title　Raw Sludge Manager

Department   Sludge Inwards
Reporting to   Raw Sludge Director

Purpose
To build, foster and direct an efficient recovery service by means of close liaison with existing customers and promoting new business, in order that stocks of raw sludge are maintained at consistently high levels, thereby enabling the Fizz-Gas Department and Organic Biscuits Department to fulfil their production targets.

Duties
(a) To establish and execute raw sludge purchases programmes in accordance with approved policies laid down by the board.

(b) To assign sludge recovery operatives as and where required, to carry out regular appraisals of individual operatives' performance, and to ensure that all recovery operations are conducted as necessary to bring results into line with objectives.

(c) To organize and administer procedures affecting raw sludge purchases, payments, terms and discounts for Class One effluent and bulk piggery collections.

(d) To plan, organize and conduct regular meetings for the purpose of instructing and motivating all raw sludge recovery personnel in the importance and technicalities of their work.

(e) To devise and maintain an adequate recruitment, selection and training programme for raw sludge recovery personnel.

(f) To devise policies and methods relative to the more efficient recovery of raw sludges, animal/chemical effluents and other waste products.

(g) To undertake regular reviews of tanker vehicle and sludge pump operating schedules.

(h) To assist senior management in the preparation of advertising and other publicity programmes.

(i) To direct the production of monthly sludge purchase forecasts and reports, sludge recovery analyses; and to make comparisons of forecasts with actual purchases as and when required by the Raw Sludge Director.

(j) To correspond and generally liaise with customers as and when required.

Responsibilities

(a) To devise and recommend to the Raw Sludge Director policies, programmes and improvements relating to:
  (i) departmental manning, organization and administration;
  (ii) the acquisition, utilization, maintenance and disposal of vehicles and other equipment;
  (iii) raw sludge purchasing prices;
  (iv) purchasing objectives;
  (v) remuneration and other benefits for departmental employees;
  (vi) departmental forecasts, operating statements and budgets.

(b) To control and direct a workforce of 1 Foreman, 3 Chargehands, 6 Drivers and 13 Raw Sludge Operatives.

Relationships

Reporting to the Raw Sludge Director, the job-holder has functional relationships with all company departments, including Fizz-Gas and Organic Biscuits Production, Sales, Accounts and Personnel; attends weekly Management Meetings.

Physical conditions

A private office is provided for the use of the job-holder within the Sludge Inwards Department, situated adjacent to the sludge pulverizing section. Hours of attendance will be 8.30 a.m. to 5.30 p.m. Monday to Friday, inclusive. As an executive of the company, the job-holder will be required to work such reasonable periods of unpaid overtime as are deemed necessary in the efficient performance of his duties.

Due to the particular conditions pertaining within the Sludge Inwards Department during hot weather, an electric fan and respirator are provided for the job-holder's personal use.

Organization details

The Raw Sludge Manager is responsible for all Sludge Inwards personnel; with the exception of the Sludge R & D Manager and two R & D Assistants, who report directly to the Raw Sludge Director.

Remuneration and other benefits

Salary range £8,700 – £10,500. The job-holder is eligible for free membership of BUPA after ten years' qualifying service. Annual holiday entitlement: 21 working days plus public holidays (or appropriate time off in lieu).

Recruitment advertising

More often than not, the business of advertising a vacancy is carried out in conditions of near-panic – or, if you prefer it, in 'wanted yesterday' conditions of dire urgency. Be that as it may, whatever the time constraints or urgency, there is simply no excuse for ignoring the four aims of effective recruitment advertising:

1   To obtain an *appropriate* response – i.e., to attract the right people for the job;
2   To provide a wholly adequate description of the post and the relevant terms of employment – expressed in clear, concise and attractive terms;

3   To present an advertisement which, overall, enhances the company image;
4   To achieve the correct choice of publication – and the best timing, position and size of advert within that publication.

So far as drafting/designing the advertisement is concerned, here is a checklist of handy tips.

Drafting/designing a recruitment advert – Checklist (65)

(*a*)   Always ensure that display advertisements carry the company logo.

(*b*)   Like it or not, the company name should not be used as the prominent 'eye-catcher' at the top of the advert – place the (informative) job title there, instead.

(*c*)   Bearing in mind that the text of the advert should provide an adequate description of the job, avoid meaningless clichés like the plague. There is no place in the advert for such horrors as:

'Pleasant and congenial working conditions'

'. . . as a member of a hard-working and dedicated team . . .'

'. . . within a highly successful, go-ahead and forward-looking company . . .'

Concentrate on actual details of the job, pay, career prospects, and so on.

(*d*)   Avoid 'blinkered' references to pay – 'salary according to age and experience,' 'circa £9,500,' etc.

(*e*)   State clearly what form of reply is required, and the closing date for applications.

Recruitment advertisement – Sample 1 (66)

SMALL BUSINESS ADVISOR
(ETHNIC MINORITIES)

£12,000

We are seeking to recruit a successful business person or manager with experience of small businesses and their development. A sound understanding of marketing, accounting, financial control and related matters is essential. You should possess demonstrable counselling skills and an appreciation of the problems encountered by members of Asian and Afro-Caribbean communities.

An application form and further details are available from the Director of Community Services, Gloamshire County Council, Shire Hall, Park Street, Newtown NN3 4FD (Tel: Newtown [4523] 77654, Ext 223).

Closing date 13 August
An Equal Opportunity Employer

GLOAMSHIRE COUNTY COUNCIL

Recruitment advertisement – Sample 2   (67)

WORKSHOP MANAGER
(AVIONICS)

Salary £11,500

Applicants should be capable of directing the work of the largest section of the plant producing avionics components for the aircraft industry. Experience in stock control procedures, production planning and CPA is essential. The successful applicant will be directly responsible for the control of 8 foremen/chargehands, 130 skilled operatives, 10 QC inspectors and 6 office staff.

Preferred age 35–40 with at least five years management/senior supervisory experience in avionics production. Membership of the IIM or IPC desirable.

Application forms and further particulars are available from the Personnel Manager, Sparkes Avionics Ltd, The Park, Mudgeley, Staffs MY6 1NN (Tel: Mudgeley [0876] 854128).

SPARKES AVIONICS LTD   *We keep them flying*

Acknowledging applications for employment

There is a growing and quite evil tendency among employers to only acknowledge those applications for employment which look 'worthwhile'. This is not only discourteous in the extreme, but totally unfeeling, to boot. Any applicant for employment (and that includes those who write in 'on spec', as well as the poor souls who don't stand a snowball's chance in hell of being accepted) deserves nothing less than a polite, nicely-worded reply. It's wise to remember that applicants who receive rude treatment at the hands of a prospective employer will not keep their feelings to themselves – they'll become damning ambassadors for the company in no time flat, and broadcast their indictment far and wide for all to hear.

A 'no-go' reply to a cold-canvas application for employment – Sample 1 (68)

Dear Miss Kludge

Thank you for your letter of 15 March expressing an interest in working for this company.

I am very sorry to tell you that we have no suitable vacancies at present. I do hope that this will not be too much of a disappointment, and would like to take this opportunity to wish you well in your search for [*alternative*] employment.

Yours sincerely

J H Wiggins
Personnel Manager

A 'no-go' reply to a cold-canvas application for employment – Sample 2 (69)

Dear Mr Paddywack

Thank you for your letter of 23 April expressing an interest in employment within this company.

Sadly, we have no suitable vacancies at present. However, I have made a note of your valuable [*inter-*

esting] qualifications and experience — and, in the event that a likely vacancy does crop up in the near future, will certainly write to you again. In this context, perhaps you would kindly let me know if you no longer wish your details to be retained on our file.

With all good wishes for your success,

Yours sincerely

P H Hackett
Personnel Manager

An interim 'hold-off' reply to an application for employment (70)

Dear Mr Fenshawe

Thank you for your application for the vacant post of .... within this company.

As you may appreciate, there has been a very heavy response to our advertisement, and it will be several days [*a week or more*] before I am in a position to advise you on the outcome.

In the meantime, I would like to thank you for your interest in our company.

Yours sincerely

F C Widgett
Personnel Manager

Rejecting the hoi-polloi

Rejection of an application for employment –
Sample 1 (71)

Dear Mrs Cringe

Thank you for your application for the post of ....
within this company. [*As promised in my letter of
***........, I now write to tell you that we have completed**
our review of all the applications for the post of
.... within this company.]**

Sadly, I have to inform you that, following the most
careful consideration, we are unable to take your
application further on this occasion.

I do hope that this letter will not be too much of a
disappointment, and would like to take the opport-
unity to wish you every success in your search for
suitable [*alternative*] employment.

Yours sincerely

C E Pomfret
Personnel Manager

Rejection of an application for employment –
Sample 2 (72)

Dear Mr Suvorov

Thank you for your most interesting application for
the appointment of .... within this company. [*As
*promised in my letter of ...., I now write to tell you**

*that we have completed our review of all the appli-
cations for the appointment of .... within this
company.]*

I am very sorry to inform you that, despite the most
careful consideration of your wide qualifications
and experience, your application has not been
successful on this occasion. [*However, I have made a
careful note of your interest – and, in the event that
a likely vacancy does crop up in the near future, will
certainly write to you again. In this context, perhaps you would kindly let me know if you no longer
wish your details to be retained on our file.*]

I do hope that this letter will not be too much of a
disappointment, and would like to wish you every
success in your search for suitable [*alternative*]
employment.

Yours sincerely

D R Jockstrap
Personnel Manager

Calling for interview

The business of waiting for, and finally being interviewed for
a job is stressful enough – so why add to a candidate's tension
by sending the poor creature a call-for-interview letter that
reads more like a summons to the Spanish Inquisition?
Remember the immutable provisions of Sod's Law – one fine
day in the future, that very same candidate could well be
considering *you* for a job. . . .

Invitation to attend for an employment interview – Sample (73)

Dear Miss Prim

**Thank you for your application for the post of ....
within this company. [*As promised in my letter of
.... regarding your application for the post of
..........., I now write to tell you that we have completed
our review of all the replies to our advertisement.*]**

**Having studied your very interesting application, I
would like to take things a stage further – and, to this
end, would ask that you kindly attend for an interview [*a preliminary interview*] [*a chat*] at this
office on 4 June at 2.30 p.m. Perhaps you would be
good enough to confirm with Miss White, my
secretary (Ext. 332), that you will be able to attend as
proposed.**

I look forward to meeting you in person.

Yours sincerely

**Ivor P Green
General Manager**

Rejecting interviewed applicants

I'm sorry, reader, but there's no escaping another homily on
the treatment of rejected candidates. If they are to call
themselves civilized, employers *must* spare more than a
passing thought for the guys and gals who, having sweated
their way through the Great Interview Handicap, wait with
bated breath for the postman. For goodness sake, if it's bad
news, let 'em know it in sympathetic, kindly terms – after all,
it costs absolutely nothing, and could do one hell of a lot for
your firm's reputation. But keep the letter short. . . .

Rejection of a job applicant after interview   (74)

Dear Mr Kludge

We have now completed our selection for the post of .... and, sadly, I have to tell you that your application has not been successful on this occasion.

I do hope that this will not be too much of a disappointment to you, and would like to express my thanks for your time and courtesy in attending the interview last Friday.

With very best wishes for your eventual success,

Yours sincerely

C T Higginbotham
General Manager

Offers of employment to applicants and written statements of particulars of employment

Let's kick off this section with a couple of sample letters offering employment to the lucky 'uns – but, first, I'd better explain why the two examples are pretty short and sweet. Apart from the obvious fact that they make the formal offer of a job, they're both intended to serve, in effect, as covering letters for that most important document, the written statement of particulars of employment. In the UK, a written statement of particulars of employment is required by law to be given to a full-time employee not later than 13 weeks from the date of employment. Note that the law (currently the Employment Protection [Consolidation] Act 1978, but y'know how things can change . . .) does not require the *contract of employment*, itself, to be in writing; for the very good reason that a contract can be oral or even implied, entered into the minute an applicant accepts the employer's offer of a job – if only by nodding his or her head and turning up for work.

Now, one convenient method of ensuring that the vital statement is not forgotten (and, boy, how often it is . . .) is to send it with the initial offer of employment – which means that the letter concerned need only be short and sweet. Presto – but there's more. . . . If you are one of those managers who tends to think in terms of contracts of employment, rather than the legally-required statements of particulars – well, then, why not combine the two of 'em? The sample statement which you'll find later in this section depicts (at the end of the document) the 'optional extra' which is necessary to satisfy both the law *and* your wish to clobber that new employee with a contract.

And now, having said all that, here are the sample letters.

Offer of employment to an applicant – Sample 1　(75)

Dear Miss Blandish

Following our most interesting discussion of last ...., I am pleased to offer you the post of .... within [*the* .... *Department of*] this company, commencing ....

I enclose a statement of the relevant particulars of employment for the post, but please do not hesitate to contact me in the event that you have any further queries. I should be much obliged if you would kindly confirm your acceptance of the offer in writing as soon as possible [*by next* ...., *at the latest*].

I look forward to welcoming you to the company [*and

to the start of what I am confident will be a long and mutually beneficial association].

Yours sincerely

M Teape
Personnel Manager

Offer of employment to an applicant – Sample 2   (76)

Dear Mr Harris

Following your interview of last ...., I am pleased to offer you the post of .... within [*the ....* *Department of*] this company, commencing ....

I enclose two copies of the statement of the relevant particulars of employment for the post, and should be much obliged if you would kindly confirm your acceptance of the offer by signing one copy and returning it to me as soon as possible [*by next ...., at the latest*]. Please do not hesitate to contact me in the event that you have any further queries.

I look forward to welcoming you to the company [*and to the start of what I am confident will be a long and mutually beneficial association*].

Yours sincerely

J D Lockjaw
General Manager

Written statement of particulars of employment – Skeleton (77)

The minimum details specified by law for inclusion in a written statement are:

(*a*) the names of the employer and the employee;

(*b*) the date of commencement of the employment;

(*c*) the date on which the employee's period of continuous employment began, taking into account any past employment which counts towards that period;

(*d*) the job title;

(*e*) the rate or method of calculating pay (including details of overtime pay; payment of commission, bonus, etc);

(*f*) the intervals at which remuneration is paid;

(*g*) hours of work;

(*h*) details of annual and public holiday entitlements, and holiday pay (including any entitlement to accrued holiday pay on leaving the employment);

(*i*) details of any conditions relating to sick leave and sick pay;

(*j*) details of any entitlement to pensions and membership of pension schemes;

(*k*) the periods of notice applicable to the employment;

(*l*) details of the person to whom the employee can apply if he or she wishes to appeal against any disciplinary decision relating to him or her, and how the application should be made;

(*m*) details of the person to whom the employee can apply if he or she wishes to seek redress of any grievance relating to his or her employment, and how the application should be made;

(*n*) whether a contracting-out certificate (issued under the Social Security Pensions Act 1975) is in force for the employment concerned.

Written statement of particulars of employment – Sample (78)

ALCOCK AND BROWN (RAMSEY) LTD

STATEMENT OF PARTICULARS OF EMPLOYMENT

Name ....

Date of commencement   Date of issue of
of employment ....   statement ....

1 You have been appointed [*promoted*] [*trans-
   ferred*] to the post of .... in the ....
   department of this company.

2 Your duties and responsibilities will be as detailed in the attached job description, but this job
   description should not be regarded as exclusive
   or exhaustive. There will be other occasional
   duties and requirements associated with your
   post and, in addition, as a term of your employment, you may be required to undertake various
   other duties and/or hours of work as may be
   reasonably required of you.

3 The date of commencement of your continuous
   service with this company is ....

4 Your specific terms and conditions of employment [*including certain provisions relating to
   your working conditions*] are contained in [*the
   Employees' Handbook issued by the company*]
   [*the works and other company rules*] [*as well as
   in existing collective agreements negotiated and
   agreed with the .... trade union recognized by
   this company for collective bargaining purposes
   in respect of the employment group to which you
   belong*]. [*These rules are available to you at your
   place of work displayed on notice boards or in
   other documentary form.*] [*These rules and
   agreements are available to you at your place of*

work displayed on notice boards or in other documentary form.] The company undertakes that any further changes in your terms and conditions [*will be notified to you*] [*will be entered in these documents*] within 30 days of the change.

5 Confirmation of your appointment will be subject to your satisfactory completion of .... months' probationary service.

6 [*Your current salary is £...... per year. Your working week is ...... hours. Overtime is/is not payable. Your normal working hours are ...... a.m. to ...... p.m. Monday to Friday. Your salary is paid monthly in arrears by credit transfer to the bank notified by you.*] [*Your current rate of pay is ...... per hour. Your working week is ...... hours. Your weekly wage is supplemented by ...., as detailed on the attached sheet. You are paid .... in arrears by. . . .*]

7 Your entitlement to pay during periods of sickness is. . . .

8 Your annual holiday entitlement is. . . .

9 The minimum periods of notice to which you are entitled are. . . .

10 Your position with regard to pension is set out in the explanatory booklet [*attached.*] [*available for your reference at. . . .*] There [*is*] [*is not*] a contracting-out certificate in force in respect of your employment.

11 You have a right to join a trade union and take part in its activities. [*Alternatively, DETAIL as agreed with the trade union concerned.*]

12 The disciplinary rules applicable to you are detailed in the. . . . In the event that you wish to appeal against any disciplinary decision relating to you, you should apply to the next level of management specified in the. . . .

13 If you have a grievance relating to your employment, please refer to the procedure outlined in the. . . .

[*I acknowledge receipt of a copy of the above, and hereby agree to the terms and particulars of my employment as detailed herein.*

***Signed* ....   *Date* ....]**

Executive service contracts

While it is likely that an employer who decides to issue an executive service contract to one of its managers will leave it to the legal-beagles to sort out, it may be the case (dare I say it) that you or your company secretary is not fully in the picture concerning this type of oh-so-valuable document. Here, then, offered with the best will in the world, is a sample.

Executive service contract – Sample   (79)

THIS AGREEMENT is made on the Sixteenth day of April 1986 BETWEEN Phineas Entwhistle (Northampton) Limited of Speke House, Gardens Road, Northampton (hereinafter termed 'the Company') of the one part and Toby Throgmorton Spike of 113 Acacia Villas South, Grindley, Northants of the other part.

WHEREAS Mr Spike was employed on 1st January 1986 by the Company NOW IT IS HEREBY AGREED as follows:

1   TERM   Mr Spike shall be and is hereby appointed Research and Development Manager and shall serve the Company and the Company shall employ Mr Spike as such Research and Development Manager for a term of five years with effect from the First day of May 1986 and thereinafter such employment shall continue unless and until this Agreement shall be determined by not less than six months notice in writing given by either party to the other expiring at any time after the end of such five year period.

2 DUTIES Mr Spike shall unless prevented by ill health during the continuance of this Agreement devote the whole of his time attention and abilities to the business and affairs of the Company. As such a Research and Development Manager Mr Spike shall faithfully and diligently serve the Company and competently and to the best of his ability carry out such duties of whatsoever nature and exercise such powers as are assigned to or vested in him by the Board for the time being and whether such duties and powers are in respect of the Company's own undertaking or business or the undertaking or business of any subsidiary or associated company of the Company and during the continuance of his employment hereunder Mr Spike shall always permanently reside within a radius of fifty miles of the Company's premises at Speke House, Gardens Road, Northampton. In the performance of such duties Mr Spike shall be responsible to the Board for the time being and shall in all respects conform to and comply with such directions and regulations as may be made by the Board and shall use his best endeavours to promote the interests of the Company. Provided that with regard to the foregoing the Board may delegate to any Managing Director of the Company for the time being or other chief executive or manager duly authorized by the Board to make any of such directions and regulations as aforesaid.

3 SALARY With effect from the 1st May 1986 there shall be paid to Mr Spike as remuneration for his services hereunder a fixed salary at the rate of £14,500 per annum or such higher rate as may from time to time be agreed between the Parties or be determined upon and notified to Mr Spike by the Company which shall review such salary annually such fixed salary to be inclusive of any fees if any payable to Mr Spike as a Director of the Company or of any subsidiary or associated company. Such salary shall accrue from day to day and shall be payable by equal monthly instalments on the last day of every month.

4   PENSION AND OTHER BENEFITS   The Company shall admit or procure the admission of Mr Spike to membership of the Company's Pension Scheme in accordance with the rules thereof for the time being and the Company will provide Mr Spike with other such employee benefits to which Mr Spike would normally be entitled as an employee of the Company.

5   TRAVEL AND EXPENSES   The Company shall provide Mr Spike with the use of a motor car in accordance with the Company's executive car policy for the time being in force. The Company shall reimburse to Mr Spike all travelling and other expenses necessarily incurred by him on behalf of the Company in the proper execution of his duties hereunder.

6   HOLIDAYS   Mr Spike shall be entitled in each year to not less than 21 working days paid holiday in addition to the normal Bank and public holidays to be taken at such reasonable time or times as may be approved by the Board. This minimum may be increased in accordance with any general holiday policy that the Company may promulgate. On the determination of Mr Spike's employment for whatever reason he shall be entitled to accrued holiday pay in direct proportion to his length of service hereunder during the calendar year in which the termination takes place. Mr Spike shall have no entitlement to any further period of holiday with or without remuneration unless mutually agreed with the Company.

7   MEDICAL EXAMINATION   During his employment hereunder Mr Spike will undergo an annual medical examination at the Company's expense and by such Doctor as the Company shall nominate and any report of such examination shall be made to the Company by such Doctor and shall remain the property of the Company.

8   SECRECY Mr Spike shall not either during the currency of this Agreement or thereafter without the consent of the Board being first obtained divulge to any person whatsoever or use for the benefit of anyone other than the Company or its subsidiary and associated companies any secrets of the Company or any confidential research information and design techniques of a confidential nature or any confidential information concerning the business accounts or finance of the Company or its subsidiary or associated companies or any of its or their transactions or affairs which may have come to his knowledge during the course of his service with the Company or with any such subsidiary or associated company as aforesaid. And in addition Mr Spike shall use his best endeavours to prevent the publication or disclosure of any such secrets research information design techniques or information as aforesaid. All records and documents made by Mr Spike or in his possession relating to the matters aforesaid shall be and remain the property of the Company or of its subsidiary or associated companies as the case may be and Mr Spike shall hand the same over to the Company at any time on demand and in any event on the termination of his employment hereunder.

9   INVENTIONS If Mr Spike shall during the continuance of this Agreement invent or discover any process or invention relating to the businesses of the Company or its subsidiary or associated companies or become possessed of any such invention or discovery it shall become the property of the Company and Mr Spike at the request and expense of the Company shall do all acts and things necessary for obtaining a patent or patents for the same if patentable or otherwise making the same available to the Company.

10   NON-SOLICITATION

(a) Upon the termination of his employment here-

under for whatever reason **Mr Spike** shall not
whether as principal servant or agent:

(i)   for a period of two years from the date of
        such termination solicit in competition
        with the Company or any of its subsidiary
        companies the custom of any person firm or
        company who at any time during the 24
        months ending upon the date of such termin-
        ation shall have been a customer of the
        Company or any of its subsidiary companies;

(ii)   for a period of two years from the date of
        such termination in competition with any
        associated company of the Company solicit
        the custom of any person firm or company
        who at any time during the 24 months ending
        upon the date of such termination shall have
        been a customer of such associated company
        and shall have been a customer with whom
        Mr Spike shall have been in contact in
        respect of such service in the performance
        of his duties hereunder at any time during
        the said period of 24 months ending upon the
        date of such termination;

(b) **Mr Spike** hereby agrees that he will not after
the termination of his employment hereunder
either personally or by his agent directly or in-
directly:

(i)   at any time represent himself as being in
        any way connected with or interested in the
        business of the Company or the business of
        any of its subsidiary or associated com-
        panies;

(ii)   at any time use or disclose to any person
        firm or company any confidential inform-
        ation directly relating to the affairs of the
        Company or any of its subsidiary or associ-
        ated companies or of any customer of the
        Company or of any such subsidiary or associ-
        ated company which may have been ac-
        quired by him in the course of or incidental

to his employment by the Company or by any
of its subsidiary or associated companies or
of any such customer as aforesaid;

(iii) for a period of 12 months after the termination of his employment hereunder either
on his own account or for any other person
firm or company solicit interfere with or
endeavour to entice away from the Company
or from any of its subsidiary or associated
companies any employee of the Company or
any of its subsidiary or associated companies as aforesaid.

11 **NO OTHER EMPLOYMENT** During the continuance of this Agreement Mr Spike shall not
without the consent of the Board directly or in-
directly be engaged concerned or interested in any
other business or occupation whatsoever either
alone or jointly with or as a Director Manager Agent
or Employee of any person firm or company. Provided that nothing in this clause shall preclude Mr
Spike from being the beneficial owner of shares
which confer on their holder up to a maximum of 10
per cent of the votes at any General Meeting of a
company any part of whose share or loan capital is
quoted or regularly dealt in on a recognized Stock
Exchange.

12 **PURCHASE AND SALE OF SHARES** Mr Spike
shall not sell or purchase any shares stock warrants
loan stock or other securities of the Company or of
its holding company or subsidiary or associated
companies except during the following times:

(i) the ten days following the publication of any
Annual Report and Accounts or half-yearly
or quarterly Reviews of any such company;

(ii) the ten days following the Annual General
Meeting of any such company.

Without prejudice to the generality of the foregoing
prohibition Mr Spike shall report to the Company
any purchase or acquisition or sale or transfer or

other disposal by himself or his spouse and/or children of any such stock warrants shares or loan stock or other securities and Mr Spike shall not make any such purchase or sale at any time when he has any confidential or privileged knowledge or information of any impending development that might affect the price of such shares stock warrants or loan stock or other securities.

13   **TERMINATION**   If Mr Spike shall during the continuance of this Agreement by reason of any bodily or mental infirmity or by accident ill health or otherwise become permanently unfitted for the proper discharge of his duties hereunder or become incapacitated from properly discharging such duties by attending business for six calendar months in any one year the Company shall be at liberty by notice in writing addressed to Mr Spike thereupon to determine this Agreement forthwith. Notwithstanding anything hereinbefore contained and in addition thereto the Company shall be at liberty to terminate Mr Spike's employment forthwith at any time during the term of this Agreement by notice in writing and addressed to him if he shall be adjudicated bankrupt or compound with his creditors or be guilty of any fraud or dishonest or serious misconduct in circumstances that would make him unsuitable to act as a Research and Development Manager of the Company or of any serious breach or non-observance of any of the conditions of this Agreement. Provided always that if his employment shall be determined by reason of his conviction or prosecution for any offence other than fraud or dishonest misconduct but not otherwise he shall be entitled to such written notice as the Board consider suitable such notice not being less than 180 days.

14   **COMPANY RECONSTRUCTION**   If before the expiration of this Agreement the employment of Mr Spike hereunder shall be terminated by reason of the liquidation of the Company for the purpose of

amalgamation of the undertaking of the Company not involving liquidation or the hiving-off of the business and part of the undertaking of the Company to a wholly owned subsidiary company or associated company and Mr Spike shall be offered employment with the amalgamated or reconstructed company or with the wholly owned subsidiary company or with such an associated company for a period of not less than the then unexpired term of this Agreement and on terms not less favourable than the terms of this Agreement Mr Spike shall have no claim against the Company in respect of the determination of his employment by the Company as hereunder.

15 EMPLOYMENT PROTECTION (CONSOLID-ATION) ACT 1978 For the purposes of the Employment Protection (Consolidation) Act 1978 Mr Spike is hereby given written notice of the following matters:

(a) There is a non-contributory pension scheme in operation called Phineas Entwhistle (Northampton) Pension Scheme of which Mr Spike will be entitled to become a member as from 1st May 1987. Full details of the scheme are contained in the booklet already handed to Mr Spike;

(b) Mr Spike has the right to belong to a trade union including the right to participate in its activities and/or become an officer thereof. Mr Spike also has the right to elect not to belong to a trade union;

(c) Mr Spike should refer any grievance about his employment hereunder to the Production Director and the reference will be dealt with by that executive or in the event that the matter cannot be resolved at that level it will be referred to the Chief Executive for final resolution;

(d) Mr Spike's hours of work shall be such hours as may be requisite for the proper discharge of his duties hereunder.

16   RESIGNATON AS DIRECTOR ON TERMINATION OF EMPLOYMENT   Should Mr Spike at any time be appointed a Director of the Company he shall not resign or be removed as a Director of the Company subject as provided hereunder during the continuance of this Agreement but upon the termination of his employment hereunder howsoever determined he shall immediately tender his resignation as a Director to the Board without prejudice to any other rights accruing to either party hereto.

17   PERFORMANCE   The failure of the Company to require or enforce the observance or performance by Mr Spike of any of the stipulations or obligations on his part herein contained shall in no way affect the right of the Company to enforce the same thereafter.

18   CANCELLATION OF PREVIOUS AGREEMENT
This Agreement is in substitution for and supersedes all previous contracts of service and arrangements whether written oral or implied between the Company and Mr Spike relating to the service of Mr Spike hereunder or between Mr Spike and any subsidiary or associated company all which Agreements and arrangements shall be deemed to have been terminated by mutual consent as from the date on which this Agreement is deemed to have commenced.

19   ARBITRATION   In case of any dispute arising between the parties hereto as to the construction of this Agreement or the rights duties or obligations of either party hereunder or any matter arising out of or concerning the same or Mr Spike's employment hereunder every such dispute or matter of difference shall be referred to a single arbitrator to be agreed between the Company and Mr Spike or in default of such agreement to be appointed on the application of either the Company or Mr Spike by the President of the Law Society for the time being. Any such arbitrator shall be deemed to be acting as an expert and not as an arbitrator and his decision shall be final and binding on the parties hereto.

20 INTERPRETATION In this Agreement the following expressions shall have the meanings assigned to them herein:

(a) 'The Board': The Directors of the Company present at a meeting of the Directors or of a Committee of the Directors duly convened and held;

(b) 'Subsidiary': Any Company which for the time being is a subsidiary company as such expression is defined by Section 154 of the Companies Act 1948 of the Company;

(c) 'Associated Company': Any Company which for the time being is a holding company as such expression is defined by Section 154 of the Companies Act 1948 of the Company or any subsidiary of any such holding company;

(d) 'The United Kingdom': The United Kingdom of Great Britain and Northern Ireland the Isle of Man and the Channel Islands.

21 LAW This Agreement shall be subject to the law of England.

22 NOTICES Any notice required to be given here-under shall be in writing and shall be deemed to be sufficiently served by either party on the other party if such notice is either delivered personally or sent by prepaid first class recorded delivery post and addressed to the party to whom such notice is to be given in the case of Mr Spike at his last known place of abode in the United Kingdom and in the case of the Company at its registered office and any such notice if so posted shall be deemed served on the day following that on which it was posted.

AS WITNESS whereof, the parties have hereunto set their hands the day and year first above written.

The Common Seal of Phineas Entwhistle (Northampton) Limited was hereto affixed in the presence of:

.... Director
.... Secretary

Signed by the said Mr Spike in the presence of:
Signature ....
Address ....
....
Occupation ....

O

....

7   Praise, beautiful praise . . .

While any sensible person knows that praise, like everything else, should be used in moderation, there are some managers who interpret this sterling principle as meaning that it should be meted out like gold-dust – and never, ever in writing. It's to be hoped, reader, that you're not one of them.

Provided one sticks like glue to the maxim, 'praise where praise is due', a carefully worded commendation is one of the finest weapons in the management armoury; it raises morale ten-fold – and, even more important, fans that proverbial fire in the belly, motivating the recipient to take on bigger and better things.

Praising the individual for a job well done

One useful tip to bear in mind is that, for full effect, a written commendation should always take the form of a personal letter to the individual concerned – an internal memo, being so commonplace in the daily round, lacks impact and tends to cheapen the exercise.

Individual praise for good effort – Sample 1   (80)

Dear Brian

Although it is only [*a matter of a fortnight*] since you were tasked with sorting out the [*appalling muddle in No 2 Store*], it is plain [*from the comments I have received*] that your efforts have already resulted in a colossal [*very significant*] [*significant*] [*marked*] improvement [*– particularly where* (*obsolete stock*) *is concerned*].

Congratulations – keep up the good work!

Yours sincerely

Arthur Mellish
Production Director

Individual praise for good effort – Sample 2   (81)

Dear Mary

The fact that last Friday's party [*the annual shindig*] was such a resounding success is due in no small part to your sterling efforts in organizing the event.

I know that this caused you much additional work – and I cannot let the occasion pass without expressing my [*personal*] thanks and gratitude.

[*Very well done!*]

Yours sincerely

C Sittingbull
Managing Director

Individual praise for good effort – Sample 3   (82)

Dear Charles

**During the last few [*weeks*] your team [*section*]
[*department*] has coped extremely well under very
difficult conditions [*considerable pressure*] – and I
know that this is largely due to the manner in which
you have motivated [*and encouraged*] all concerned
to give of their best.**

Congratulations – keep up the good work!

Yours sincerely

F D Dogsbody
Sales Director

Laudatory appraisal narratives

Laudatory appraisal reports – Phrase-bank   (83)

> **. . .a keen and energetic member of staff. . .**
> **. . .dependable, enthusiastic and hard-working. . .**
> **. . .eminently loyal and dedicated to. . .**
> **. . .has displayed a commendable acumen. . .**
> **. . .hard-working, dedicated and loyal. . .**
> **. . .reflecting a maturity beyond his [*her*] years. . .**
> **. . .has more than justified my faith in. . .**
> **. . .has exceeded all my expectations. . .**
> **. . .has proved beyond all doubt that. . .**
> **. . .has borne a very considerable workload with. . .**
> **. . .unflagging enthusiasm and dedication to the task. . .**

. . .commendable enthusiasm and a determination to succeed. . .

. . .a credit to the company. . .

. . .has achieved outstandingly good results. . .

. . .has achieved excellent results. . .

. . .has achieved commendable results. . .

. . .has performed outstandingly well. . .

. . .has performed excellently. . .

. . .has performed very well. . .

. . .capable of sustained and commendable effort. . .

. . .has proved an outstanding success. . .

. . .has set an example. . .

. . .sound, reliable and hard-working. . .

. . .displays excellent qualities of management. . .

. . .reflecting an innate flair for good management. . .

. . .by dint of sheer hard work. . .

. . .an understanding and perceptive manager. . .

. . .sterling qualities and capabilities. . .

. . .admired and respected by his [*her*] staff. . .

. . .at his [*her*] best under pressure. . .

. . .eminently suited to the appointment. . .

. . .who much enjoys his [*her*] work. . .

. . .is worthy of the highest commendation. . .

. . .enjoys hard work. . .

. . .arriving early and departing late. . .

. . .ever-punctual. . .

. . .much unpaid overtime. . .

. . .works hard and long. . .

. . .self-disciplined and capable. . .

. . .caring and considerable manager. . .

. . .enjoys meeting and beating a challenge. . .

. . .delegates wisely and well. . .

. . .always keen to accept responsibility. . .

. . .authoritative but never coercive. . .

. . .wielding a quiet but firm authority. . .

. . .a firm but eminently fair disciplinarian. . .

. . .quietly authoritative. . .

. . .displays commendable tact and patience. . .

. . .at his [*her*] best when dealing with people. . .

. . .a sound and able negotiator. . .

. . .has earned the respect of. . .

. . .displays considerable skill as a negotiator. . .

. . .an effective and sympathetic counsellor. . .

. . .a highly proficient and perceptive interviewer. . .

. . .an eminently professional approach. . .

. . .thrives on responsibility. . .

. . .eminently suited for promotion. . .

. . .qualified in every respect for. . .

. . .merits the most serious consideration. . .

. . .my fear is, we may lose him [*her*]. . .

. . .[*long*] overdue for promotion. . .

. . .is worthy of, and is seeking advancement. . .

Laudatory appraisal report – Sample narrative (84)

I am pleased to report that John has performed exceptionally well since his promotion to Department Manager some nine months ago. The branch has been beset with a number of difficulties during this time – significantly, the move of premises and recurrent industrial relations problems – and I have been impressed by the manner in which he has not allowed these to occlude his innate flair for sound and practical management.

Bearing in mind that this is his first executive appointment, he has achieved a notably successful working relationship with his staff and it is plain that he enjoys their respect – and their confidence. Without doubt, one of his most impressive achievements during the period was the skill with which he tackled and solved the various causes of unrest within the department that greeted him on his arrival in post – thereby earning for himself an

early reputation as a perceptively practical and
fair-minded manager.

So far as his technical skills are concerned, I regard
John as a first-class administrator. Taking advantage of the move of premises to reorganize much of
his department's work, he has achieved some note-
worthy economies — and it is very much to his credit
that his bailiwick is now operating within budget for
the first time in over three years.

In sum, an excellent performance.

L F Carruthers
Director of Administration

Notifications of increases in pay

Notification of increase in salary – Sample 1 (85)

Dear Sheila

This year's salary review has now been completed,
and I am pleased to inform you that your salary will
be [*has been*] increased by £.......... to £.......... per
annum, with effect from .... 198....

Keep up the good work!

Yours sincerely

S D J Marner
General Manager

Notification of increase in salary – Sample 2   (86)

Dear Sheila

I am very pleased to inform you that, in recognition of your splendid performance during the past twelve months, your salary will be [*has been*] increased by £...... to £........ per annum, with effect from .... 198....

[*You have certainly earned this increase – keep up the good work!*]

Yours sincerely

S D J Marner
General Manager

Notifications of promotion

Notification of promotion – Sample 1   (87)

Dear June

It gives me much pleasure to inform you that your recent application for the post of Credit Controller has been successful, and that your well-earned promotion will take effect from 1 July 1986.

[*Needless to say, I have every confidence in your ability to meet and beat this new challenge – and look forward to your joining our team.*] [*Congratulations – and welcome to the team!*]

Yours sincerely

D R Grimsdyke
Group Accountant

Notification of promotion – Sample 2   (88)

Dear Maurice

As you will doubtless be aware, Ken Livingstone's recent departure [*promotion*] [*sad death*] [*impending retirement*] has created [*will create*] a vacancy in our Area Manager team.

Your splendid efforts and overall standards of performance over the past three years convince me that you would make a first-class replacement for Ken, and it is with much pleasure that I now formally offer you the post of Area Manager (Eastern Region).

Naturally, it is my hope that you will accept this offer – but, since I am sure there are many matters you would like to discuss before reaching a final decision, I think it would be a good idea if you come for a chat on 20 June at 10.30 a.m.

With all good wishes,

Yours sincerely

H D Peebles
Sales Director

Round-robin praise

When it comes to handing out 'corporate' praise, one common, tactical error committed by many bosses is to shower the leader of the team concerned with laudatory comment – and then spoil it all by adding the rider, 'Please convey my thanks and appreciation to all concerned for this splendid effort'. Bearing in mind that, in the vast majority of cases, it's the poor bloody Indians who've *done* all the work, this is a particularly lazy approach – and, while personalized letters to all and sundry may be out of the question, the round-robin memo is most certainly not. So, think on't. . . .

Round-robin praise – Sample 1 (89)

INTERNAL MEMORANDUM

TO **All Sales Staff**   DATE **14 May 86**

FROM **Sales Director**   REF **FG/231/22**

THE PADDYWACK CAMPAIGN

As you know, the Paddywack launch has now been completed – and I cannot let the occasion pass without expressing my sincere thanks for the manner in which each and every one of you contributed to its resounding success. A magnificent total of 12,750 Paddywack Kits were sold during the fortnight, and our production colleagues are now frantically trying to meet the extraordinary further demand which has been generated by *your* efforts.

Congratulations on a magnificent achievement!

FG
Sales Director

Round-robin praise – Sample 2   (90)

INTERNAL MEMORANDUM

TO   **All Members of Staff**   DATE   **27 Mar 86**

FROM   **Pers Mgr**   REF   **PM/43/12**

Thanks to the sterling effort made by each and every one of you, the move to our new accommodation has been completed with an absolute minimum of fuss and disruption. I am very conscious that you have all suffered considerable inconvenience over the past few days, and it is very much to your credit that you have not allowed this to affect your work – or dampen your habitual enthusiasm!

Once again, my sincere thanks.

**CHG
Pers Mgr**

Round-robin praise – Sample 3   (91)

INTERNAL MEMORANDUM

TO   **All Members of Staff**   DATE   **9 Apr 86**

FROM   **G I Floggem**   REF   **HoD/14/5**

HMI's VISIT

I have now received the HMI's report on his recent visit to the College and wish you all to know that, once again, we have received nothing but laudatory comment. Needless to say, this continued success in the face of mounting difficulties and constraints is entirely due to the sterling efforts made by each and every one of you – and I cannot let the occasion pass without expressing my very sincere gratitude, and my pride in your achievement.

I shall be circulating relevant extracts of the HMI's report to all concerned – but, in the meantime, my congratulations and thanks to you all.

GIF
HoD

Valedictory letters to retirees

Valedictory letters to retirees – Guidelines (92)

1 Do not dwell overlong in the letter on the subject of old Bert's past service – merely allude to the years spent in harness and, if you must, highlight one of his peak achievements.

2 Try to avoid undue solemnity. After all, whatever Bert may think to the contrary, retirement is supposed to be a celebration – so don't make your letter read like a funeral oration.

3 By all means, congratulate Bert on his retirement, but *never* wish him luck – in his frame of mind, he doesn't wish to be reminded that the retirement gamble is the last shake of the dice. . . .

4 If you have any possible use for Bert's talents on a part-time or occasional consultancy basis, then refer to this in

the letter – *and mean what you say.*

5   Don't hand Bert the letter at his farewell presentation;
    send it by post to his home address, timed to arrive on or
    shortly after the first day of his retirement – and make no
    mention of it during the get-together.

Valedictory letter to retiree – Sample   (93)

Dear Bert

**Retirement presentations [*parties*] tend – on the
surface, at least – to be informal and light-hearted
affairs. So, albeit that I took great pleasure in saying
the traditional 'few words' at your get-together, I
now write in serious vein to express my [*our*] very
sincere appreciation for all that you have done
during your .... years' service with the company.**

**[*Knowing you as I do, I am absolutely certain that
you will tackle the opportunities presented by
retirement (so-called 'retirement') with the same
zeal and energy which you so constantly displayed
when in harness – and thus make a mockery of the
belief held by some sad-sacks that it's a time for
sitting back!*]**

**[*I'm naturally very pleased that we are going to
continue our relationship on a part-time (consultancy) (an occasional) basis, and look forward
to ....*]**

**Again, my congratulations [*to both you and Mary*] –
and my grateful thanks.**

Yours sincerely

Frank Globb

Commending suppliers for good service

Oh, yes, and why not? How many times do *you* receive laudatory letters from satisfied customers – and on those rare occasions, aren't you made to feel just a little warm inside? There's nothing like such a thank-you from this or that customer to make you think that, just perhaps, it's all been worth-while – and if the self-same guy or gal subsequently asks a favour, you'll probably bend over backwards to help, won't you? So, placing the boot firmly on the other foot, when one of your suppliers really comes up trumps, write and tell him or her so – believe me, it's good self-insurance.

Commending a supplier for good service – Sample 1 (94)

Dear Mr Allison

Our Order No ....

The purpose of this note is to express my appreciation for the very prompt manner in which you fulfilled our urgent order. In business, brickbats fly like confetti – so, just for a change, please accept my thanks!

Yours sincerely

**F Splurge
Purchasing Manager**

Commending a supplier for good service –
Sample 2   (95)

Dear Mr Phipps

As you will know, we are one of your regular customers – and, as such, I think it is high time that we expressed our thanks for the consistently prompt and caring manner in which you have attended to our requirements.

We really appreciate your commendable standards of service.

Yours sincerely

J G Glossop
Purchasing Manager

8 Disciplinary bits an' bobs

And this is where the 'wretched finger 'aving writ' homily really does come into play – for if there's one type of writing that's sure-fire certain to bounce back and clobber yer average manager straight between the eyes, it's all that stuff he pens on discipline. If you, reader, have ever experienced the dubious pleasures of an industrial tribunal hearing – well, 'tis likely you'll know exactly what I mean. It can be an unpleasant experience to have one's old and forgotten paperwork dissected and denounced by the other side – who, scenting blood, are hell-bent on convincing the tribunal that the creature appearing before 'em is a tyrant or an idiot. Or both . . .

Disciplinary writing – The golden rules (96)

1 Having drafted whatever it is, consider *every word* in terms of its contribution to the whole – and mercilessly slash any superfluities.
2 Examine the sequence and logicality of the result. Does it say *exactly* what you are trying to say – no more, no less – in an unimpeachable format and style?
3 Then, right at the moment when you're satisfied that everything in the garden is lovely, submit the piece to the most stringent test of all. . . . Does it reflect the *whole* truth, present *all* the facts – without wandering off into *supposition?*

4   And, no, you're not off the hook, yet. The 'finished' piece
    may fit the requirements of the present situation in every
    conceivable way — but does it contain any latent pitfalls
    for the future? For instance, have you, in effect, compiled
    your own tribunal death warrant?

    Then, and only then, can you say — publish and be
    damned!

'I'm disappointed in you' themes

Admonitory letter – Sample   (97)

Dear Charles

**As you will know, yesterday morning, while on my
way to an appointment in Tavistock, I called at your
office purely on the off-chance of seeing you — and,
quite naturally, was not at all put out when Sally told
me that I had missed you by only a few minutes.**

**However, what did concern me was the state of your
reception area — which, judging by the condition of
the carpet, the amount of dust on the furniture and
overall untidiness, was in sore need of a thorough
cleaning. This is plainly not good enough, and you
are to take immediate action to ensure that the
whole of your branch is clean and presentable at all
times.**

**I find it annoying and disappointing that I should be
required to write in this vein, and I trust there will
be no further need for me to bring such an obvious
type of failing to your attention.**

Yours sincerely

**J K Doe
Sales Director**

Admonitory memo – Sample (98)

```
┌─────────────────────────────────────────────────────┐
│                                                       │
│              INTERNAL MEMORANDUM                      │
│                                                       │
├─────────────────────────────────────────────────────┤
│                                                       │
│  TO  Miss D Pulham          DATE  19 Mar 86          │
│                                                       │
│  FROM  Gen Mgr              REF  GM/14/10/6          │
│                                                       │
├─────────────────────────────────────────────────────┤
```

THE ROUTLEDGE REPORT

1 It is now some three weeks since I requested you to prepare a full report on the Routledge affair – but, despite my having reminded you on two occasions, I have yet to receive your draft.

2 Since I have heard nothing from you, I am forced to assume that there are no cogent reasons for the inordinate delay – and I find this most disappointing. You are to ensure that the completed document is on my desk by Monday morning, 24 Mar, at the latest.

GBH
Gen Mgr

```
└─────────────────────────────────────────────────────┘
```

Adverse appraisal narratives

Adverse appraisal reports – Phrase-bank (99)

. . .a lazy and lethargic member of staff. . .
. . .lacking in enthusiasm and patently idle. . .
. . .uninterested in his [*her*] work. . .
. . .has displayed little personal acumen. . .
. . .indolent and uninterested in. . .
. . .reflecting an overall immaturity. . .
. . .has not attempted to live up to. . .
. . .has disappointed me beyond measure. . .
. . .has failed to meet even the lowest stand-

ards. . .

. . .has not satisfied me that he [*she*] can. . .

. . .minimal enthusiasm or dedication to the task. . .

. . .lacking any visible determination to succeed. . .

. . .a discredit to the company. . .

. . .has achieved disgracefully poor results. . .

. . .has achieved very poor results. . .

. . .has achieved little in the way of results. . .

. . .has performed outstandingly badly. . .

. . .has put in a most disappointing performance. . .

. . .his [*her*] performance has been mediocre. . .

. . .incapable of sustained effort. . .

. . .has proved an abject failure. . .

. . .has failed to set an example. . .

. . .lacks reliability, in that. . .

. . .displays reprehensible qualities of management. . .

. . .reflecting innately poor management skills. . .

. . .by dint of avoiding, rather than tackling his [*her*] work. . .

. . .an unimaginative and stolid. . .

. . .lacking in perception and understanding. . .

. . .poor qualities and capabilities. . .

. . .feared and actively disliked by his [*her*] staff. . .

. . .is patently unable to cope under pressure. . .

. . .quite unsuited to the appointment. . .

. . .who seems to dislike his [*her*] work. . .

. . .does not merit commendation. . .

. . .actively dislikes hard work. . .

. . .arriving late and departing early. . .

. . .never [*hardly ever*] [*seldom*] punctual. . .

. . .has an antipathy to any form of overtime. . .

. . .a nine-to-five outlook. . .

. . .regards work as an unnecessary and avoidable evil. . .

...conspicuously lacking in self-discipline...

...uncaring and inconsiderate...

...seldom rises to a [*any*] challenge...

...inclined to over-delegate [*under-delegate*] work...

...guilty of over-delegating [*under-delegating*] work...

...seldom [*never*] keen to accept responsibility...

...a coercive authoritarian...

...manages by coercion...

...a harsh and intolerant disciplinarian...

...fails to maintain discipline...

...a poor disciplinarian...

...lacking in authority...

...unable to command respect...

...displays little tact or patience...

...is tactless and impatient...

...is at his [*her*] worst when dealing with people...

...an unreliable and nervous negotiator...

...lacking in negotiation skills...

...has failed to earn the respect of...

...is an inept counsellor...

...is [*totally*] unsuited to the counselling role...

...a nervous and incompetent interviewer...

...a poor interviewer, incapable of...

...a totally unprofessional approach...

...lacking in professionalism...

...fails to adequately discharge his [*her*] responsibilities...

...neither suited nor qualified for promotion at the present time...

Adverse appraisal report – Sample narrative (100)

I am bound to say that John's performance during the period under review has been worrying. As a negotiator, he is plainly much involved in the constant round of meetings and day-to-day dealings with trade union representatives, and it is in this context that I have serious reservations regarding his overall capabilities and judgement.

There have been a number of instances when he has displayed a singular lack of elementary courtesy and tact during meetings with union representatives – to the extent that, on two such occasions, I found it necessary to admonish him for his overbearing manner. Also, while I make due allowance for the oft-frustrating attitudes encountered at the negotiating table, I have not been impressed by John's apparent inability to refrain from impetous and ill-advised comment – which, at times, has most certainly not helped matters.

In addition, I am convinced that John has not achieved the necessary degree of rapport with his peers and colleagues on the negotiating team. There is no doubt that he has succeeded in annoying some members of the team – again, as a result of his propensity for injudicious, off-the-cuff comment and criticism. Plainly, this has a most disruptive effect, and is therefore a matter of some concern.

I have been unable to fault his professional knowledge or his performance in the other aspects of his job. He enjoys commendable powers of written expression, is a dedicated and painstaking researcher – and can always be relied upon to work hard and long hours without a vestige of complaint.

I have discussed the contents of this report with John, and have arranged for him to attend a fourteen-day course on negotiating skills. I have made it quite clear that I expect him to effect a marked improvement in his manner of dealing with the union representatives and his colleagues, and I have informed him that I will review the situation in three months' time.

G P Arbuthnot
Director of Industrial Relations

Formal written warnings

First formal written warning (misconduct) – Sample (101)

NOTICE OF FORMAL WARNING

To   Mr A Christian   **Job Title**   Cleaner

Dept Production   **Date**   11 March 1986

The purpose of this notice is to confirm that at a disciplinary hearing held earlier today you were adjudged guilty of misconduct; in that:

at approximately 3.45 p.m. on 10 March 1986, you were observed by Mr J B Hope, Assistant Production Manager, to be smoking a cigarette while working in the Volatile Liquids Store, a clearly-marked 'No Smoking' area — an act which was in flagrant breach of company regulations.

After full consideration of this matter, you are now warned that any repetition of misconduct on your part will place your employment with this company at risk. This warning constitutes the first formal stage of the company's disciplinary procedure. It will be recorded in your personnel record and will remain there for three months, after which it will be expunged provided that your conduct has been satisfactory during this time. You have a right of appeal against this warning. If you wish to exercise this right, you should address your appeal, within seven days of the date of this notice, to the Production Director.

T D Bligh
Production Manager

First formal written warning (incapability) –
Sample   (102)

NOTICE OF FORMAL WARNING

To   Mr I Haddit   **Job Title**   General Clerk

Dept   Administration   **Date**   11 March 1986

The purpose of this notice is to confirm that at a disciplinary hearing held earlier today you were adjudged guilty of lack of capability and care with your work; in that:

on the morning of 10 March 1986, during an inspection by Mr P Donne, Administration Supervisor, of the Confidential Registry, a classified correspondence storage area for which you are currently responsible, it was discovered by Mr Donne that five confidential files were missing. It being established by Mr Donne that you could offer no reasonable explanation or indication as to the whereabouts of this material, he then informed you that you would be reported for a breach of company security regulations.

After full consideration of this matter, you are now warned that any repetition of such failure to reach the level of performance appropriate to your duties will place your employment with this company at risk. This warning constitutes the first formal stage of the company's disciplinary procedure. It will be recorded in your personnel record and will remain there for three months, after which it will be expunged provided that your performance has been satisfactory during this time. You have a right of appeal against this warning. If you wish to exercise this right, you should address your appeal, within seven days of the date of this notice, to the Director of Administration.

J Jeffries
Administration Manager

Final written warning – Sample (103)

<u>NOTICE OF FINAL WARNING</u>

<u>To</u>   Miss E N Everready <u>Job Title</u> Copy Typist

<u>Dept</u> Typing Pool   <u>Date</u>   5 June 1986

The purpose of this notice is to confirm that at a disciplinary hearing held earlier today you were adjudged guilty of misconduct; in that:

at approximately 2.35 p.m. on 4 June 1986, you were advised by Mrs J Grimrod, Typing Pool Supervisor, that a report you had typed contained a number of serious errors. Your reply was couched in highly offensive terms, and you

were accordingly informed by Mrs Grimrod that
you would be reported for misconduct.

After full consideration of this matter, you are now
warned that any repetition of misconduct on your
part will render you liable to dismissal without
further warning. This warning constitutes the
second formal stage of the company's disciplinary
procedure. It will be recorded in your personnel
record and will remain there for three months, after
which it will be expunged provided that your conduct
has been satisfactory during this time. You have a
right of appeal against this warning. If you wish to
exercise this right, you should address your appeal,
within seven days of the date of this notice, to the
Director of Administration.

J Jeffries
Administration Manager

Notifications of summary dismissal

Notification of summary dismissal – Sample 1 (104)

NOTIFICATION OF SUMMARY DISMISSAL

To	Mr C W Flabb	**Job Title**	Mechanic
Dept	Service	**Date**	8 May 1986

Brief details and date of offence

At approximately 10.15 a.m. on 6 May 1986, you were
observed by Mr H R Himmler, Service Bay Foreman,
to remove the spare wheel from a Talbot Horizon,

Reg No. B103 RAC, the property of a customer, and place the same in the boot of your private vehicle, which you then locked. On being questioned by Mr Himmler, you admitted that it had been your intention to steal the spare wheel, and you were accordingly informed by Mr Himmler that you would be reported for gross misconduct.

After full consideration of this matter at a disciplinary hearing held earlier today, you were adjudged guilty of gross misconduct and you are, therefore, dismissed from the company's employment with immediate effect.

If you consider that you have been wrongly or unfairly dismissed you have the right to appeal. If you wish to exercise this right, you should address your appeal in writing, within three working days of your dismissal, to the Service Director.

You are requested to acknowledge receipt of this notification of summary dismissal by signing the duplicate copy.

G T Harrap
Service Manager

I acknowledge receipt of a copy of this notification.

Signed .... Date ....

Notification of summary dismissal – Sample 2 (skeleton) (105)

NOTIFICATION OF SUMMARY DISMISSAL

Name of employee **Dept** ....

Brief details and date of offence

....
....
....
....

You are notified that the above offence constituting gross misconduct has been proved and you are, therefore, dismissed from the company's employment with immediate effect.

If you consider that you have been wrongly or unfairly dismissed from your employment, you have the right to appeal. If you wish to exercise this right, you should address your appeal in writing, within three working days of your dismissal, to the ....

Name of employee's representative present during the disciplinary hearing: ....

Signed .... **Date** ....
(Person authorizing dismissal)

Signed .... **Date** ....
(Person being dismissed)

Dismissal on redundancy

Letter of dismissal on redundancy – Sample (106)

Dear Mary [*Mrs Jones*]

Further to our discussion of earlier today, it is with [*very*] much regret that I must ask you to accept this letter as formal notice of the redundancy of your post with effect from 31 August 1986.

[*The services of the Personnel Department will, of course, be available to assist you in obtaining suitable, alternative employment – and the Company will gladly grant you reasonable time off with pay for the purposes of attending job interviews or undertaking training for alternative employment.*]

You will be notified of the details of your forthcoming redundancy and severance pay within the next few days [*I enclose details of your forthcoming redundancy and severance pay*]. Please do not hesitate to speak to me [*to contact me*] in the event that I can be of any help.

On behalf of the Company, I should like to thank you [*express my warm appreciation*] for the services you have given us in the past and wish you every success in the future. [*Needless to add, I shall be only too pleased to supply any prospective employer with a reference on your behalf.*]

Yours sincerely

**K F Brotherton
Administrative Manager**

Written statements of reasons for dismissal

A dismissed employee in the good old UK is legally entitled to request his or her ex-employer to provide a written statement of the reasons for his or her dismissal. As some of us know to our cost, non-compliance with the request or the furnishing of an untrue or inaccurate statement is a splendid method of ensuring one's sweaty presence at an industrial tribunal – so, watch dem statements!

Statement of reasons for dismissal – Skeleton(107)

The law doesn't lay down a set format or list the required contents of a statement of reasons for dismissal. Here is a suggested skeleton:

(*a*)   employer's name (obviously, use of a firm's printed letter-head takes care of this one);

(*b*)   ex-employee's name, job title and department/section;

(*c*)   effective date of termination of employment;

(*d*)   statement of the reasons for dismissal (*see* Section 108);

(*e*)   signature on behalf of the employer, and date;

(*f*)   if desired, a space for the ex-employee's signature on the duplicate copy, for retention as evidence of receipt.

Written statements of reasons for dismissal – Skeleton reasons   (108)

> . . .due to your lack of capability for performing work of the kind for which you were employed (e.g. [*provide adequate details of the duties concerned*]). . .
>
> . . .due to your misconduct (e.g. [*provide the date and adequate details of the offence*]). . .
>
> . . .due to your misconduct (e.g. [*provide the date and adequate details of the offence*]) following a previous warning for misconduct. . .

...due to your gross misconduct (e.g. [*provide the date and adequate details of the offence*])...

...due to your redundancy, in that the company's requirements for work of the kind for which you were employed (i.e. [*provide adequate details of the duties concerned*]) have ceased [*diminished to the point where your job is no longer viable*] [*are expected to cease*] [*are expected to diminish to the point where your job will no longer be viable*]...

...due to the termination of your temporary contract of employment, in that the company's requirements for work of the nature for which you were temporarily employed has now ceased [*because of the lack of need on the part of the company for the post to continue to be occupied by a temporary employee*]...

Round-robin admonishments

Round-robin admonishment – Sample 1   (109)

INTERNAL MEMORANDUM			
TO	**All Members of Staff**	DATE	**5 Jun 86**
FROM	**Head of Department**	REF	**GC/13/4**

UNAUTHORIZED USE OF OFFICE COPIERS
Despite my previous instructions on the subject, it is obvious that office copiers are still being used for totally unauthorized, private purposes.

I wish to make it quite clear that I will not tolerate this continued misuse of valuable office resources and the practice is to cease forthwith.

GC
HoD

Round-robin admonishment – Sample 2   (110)

INTERNAL MEMORANDUM

<u>CONFIDENTIAL</u>

TO	Circulation List B		DATE	17 Jul 86
FROM	CD1	REF	SC/C1543/12/CD1	

<u>SECURITY OF CLASSIFIED MATERIAL</u>

A recent check of the S & C Registry has revealed that managers are still passing classified files from hand-to-hand without first notifying the registry clerk of such transfers. This practice constitutes a serious breach of security regulations and is to cease forthwith.

R G Croft
CD1

<u>CONFIDENTIAL</u>

Round-robin admonishment – Sample 3 (111)

INTERNAL MEMORANDUM

CONFIDENTIAL

TO	Members of Team Bravo (P L Harrison, J Wood, Miss F D Goldsmith)	DATE	6 Aug 86
FROM	Director, Weapons Div	REF	GM/32/2/1

DIPCON PROJECT

1 Despite your collective reassurances, during the past month there has been a marked escalation of the antipathy between the Dipcon Project staff and Team Bravo. An examination of this antipathy clearly indicates that all of you are now persona non grata where your participation in this vital project is concerned.

2 Since it is a primary function of our Support Teams to serve the various experimental groups on a basis of mutual respect and confidence, any such deterioration of working relationships prohibits the Weapons Division properly performing its role within the British Outerspace organization.

3 It is therefore with regret that I must now inform you that Team Bravo is disbanded with immediate effect. Pending your individual reallocation to alternative posts within the Division, you are each to report to Dr H Jones, Research 2a, at 10.00 a.m. on 8 August for final clearance and assignment to temporary research duties.

G Marshall
Director, Wpns Div

CONFIDENTIAL

Round-robin admonishment – Sample 4   (112)

INTERNAL MEMORANDUM

TO	**All Accounts Staff**	DATE	**20 Jun 86**
FROM	**Accts Mgr**	REF	**12.203.34**

Despite my explicit instructions to the contrary, some members of staff are still failing to clear and tidy their desks before leaving the office at the end of the day. Quite apart from aspects of security, such slipshod habits reflect badly on the department as a whole and the individuals concerned, in particular.

I wish to emphasize that I will take a most serious view of any further instances of such laxity.

KLR
Accts Mgr

Orders and instructions

If there is one thing that tends to land the average, workaday manager in hot water, it is the vexed old business of delivering orders and instructions (call 'em what you will) in the right 'style' – that is, in the manner best calculated to obtain all-round, satisfactory results. Consider, say, a simple requirement that a given task must be completed by noon on 10 July 1986, and note just some of the many ways in which this instruction can be expressed:

The work is to be completed by [*no later than*] noon on 10 July 1986.
The work will be completed by [*no later than*] noon on 10 July 1986.

The work must be completed by [*no later than*] noon on 10 July 1986.

The work should be completed by [*no later than*] noon on 10 July 1986.

You are to complete the work by [*no later than*] noon on 10 July 1986.

You will complete the work by [*no later than*] noon on 10 July 1986.

You must complete the work by [*no later than*] noon on 10 July 1986.

You should complete the work by [*no later than*] noon on 10 July 1986.

The operative [*etc.*] is to complete the work by [*no later than*] noon on 10 July 1986.

The operative [*etc.*] will complete the work by [*no later than*] noon on 10 July 1986.

The operative [*etc.*] must complete the work by [*no later than*] noon on 10 July 1986.

The operative [*etc.*] should complete the work by [*no later than*] noon on 10 July 1986.

Completion date: by [*no later than*] noon on 10 July 1986.

Plainly, the choice of style should be determind by:
(*a*) the urgency of the situation;
(*b*) the attitudes of the recipient(s);
(*c*) the complexity of the task.

However, unfortunately and all too often, the overall style of an instruction is moulded by, and thoroughly steeped in the fall-out from the personality of the manager concerned. Hence, the one hundred per cent autocratic son-of-a-gun will issue nothing but coldly-coercive commands and orders – and, going to the other end of the scale, the wee timorous beastie of a manager will wallow in the issue of pleas for action. The moral is simple and direct:

TO WHAT EXTENT DO YOUR ORDERS AND INSTRUCTIONS REFLECT YOUR PERSONALITY?

AND WHEN ARE YOU GOING TO DO SOMETHING ABOUT THIS FAILING?

Remember, prith'ee the 'descending order of the imperative':

The command   This is all fine and dandy for the parade ground, but, in business and industry, there's precious little room for commands. Reserve 'em for the dire emergencies, like fires and bomb-scares, etc.

The instruction   And here we have the happy average – or do we? The effective manager may well make good use of –

The request   Delivered in the right way to the right people, the request is often all that's required. But, of course, there are the really conscientious workers who will spring into action on receipt of nothing more than –

The suggestion   Yes, even in writing, this is often more than sufficient to produce results.

The plea   In one word, yuk. The mismanager who resorts to the plea deserves all he gets.

Orders and instructions – Sample 1   (113)

ARTIFICIAL RESPIRATION
The most effective way of giving artificial respiration, and the easiest to use, is the mouth-to-mouth (kiss of life) method of forcing air into the victim's lungs.

What to do
* **Lay the patient on his or her back.**
* **Turn his or her head to one side.**
* **Clear any obstruction from the patient's mouth.**
* **Turn his or her head upwards.**
* **Place a folded coat, or some similar object, under his or her shoulders.**
* **Angle the patient's head by pressing his or her forehead down and lifting his or her chin up.**

* Pinch his or her nostrils closed (except in the case of a small child).
* Take a deep breath.
* Cover the victim's mouth with yours (for a child, cover the nose also).
* Blow *gently.*
* Look for rising of the patient's chest.
* Remove your mouth.
* Take a deep breath while the patient's chest deflates.
* Repeat the blowing procedure *six* times *quickly*, then ten times a minute (for a child, 20 shallow breaths a minute).
* When breathing re-starts, place the patient in the recovery position (see diagram).

Orders and instructions – Sample 2 (114)

(Extract from instructions for the operation of a staff appraisal scheme.)

APPRAISAL INTERVIEWS

21.1 The assessor is to interview each member of staff being reported on as soon as possible after the appraisal form has been completed. At the outset of the interview, the appraisee is to be given a full opportunity to peruse the completed report, and should be invited to comment on the findings.

21.2 The interview should take account of any counselling already undertaken during the period under review, and must include advice and discussion on the development of the appraisee's potential as well as the correction of his/her weaknesses.

21.3 At the conclusion of the interview, the appraisee is to be invited to indicate *either* his/her acceptance of the report as written by signing the statement in Part IV, *or* enter such comment as he/she thinks fit in the space provided. In this context, it is emphasized that the assessor should make no attempt to influence the appraisee's decision or any comments that he/she may wish to make.

Orders and instructions – Sample 3 (115)

INTERNAL MEMORANDUM

TO	G Hawkes	DATE	23 May 86
	[*George Hawkes*]		
FROM	Gen Mgr	REF	CW/51/23
	[*C Williams*]		
	[*Clive Williams*]		

LAUNCH OF THE EXPEDITOR MK III

In order that I can integrate our planning, please [*I should be obliged if you would*] let me have details of any literature/brochures, etc. you intend producing for the forthcoming launch.

C W
[*C Williams*]
[*Clive Williams*]
[*Clive*]

Orders and instructions – Sample 4 (116)

INTERNAL MEMORANDUM

TO	Export Mgr [*Dick Mayhew*]	DATE	13 Aug 86
FROM	Trng Mgr [*P White*] [*Peter White*]	REF	TM/24/6/2

EXPORT DOCUMENTATION COURSE

Your memo EM/12/3 of 11 Aug 86 refers. I have made arrangements for Paul Minter to attend the DCL three-day course on export documentation to be held in London on 2–5 Sep., inclusive. I will let you have his joining instructions and accommodation details within the next few days.

Since course participants will be required to demonstrate their existing company export documentation, kindly [*please*] ensure that Minter takes with him copies of the relevant paperwork.

P W
[*P White*]
[*Peter White*]
[*Pete*]

Orders and instructions – Sample 5 (117)

STAFF INSTRUCTION 9/86

BOMB ALERTS

In the event of a bomb alert, the following 'staff message' will be broadcast over the PA system:

**'ATTENTION ALL STAFF – EXERCISE ESCORT,
REPEAT,
EXERCISE ESCORT'**

On receipt of this message, all members of staff are
to politely but firmly shepherd customers to the
nearest normal or emergency exit point. Since the
paramount need will be to evacuate the store in the
shortest possible time, any sales in course of transaction are to be abandoned and no attempt is to be
made to remove cash from, or otherwise secure tills.

Having evacuated all customers from their respect-
ive sections to the street, staff are not to re-enter the
store on any pretext whatsoever until so authorized
by the general manager or his appointed deputy.

Plainly, in order to prevent panic among customers,
it is of the utmost importance that staff respond to
the alert in a brisk and cheerful manner. Should the
occasion arise, I am confident that every member of
our team will act accordingly.

G Willoughby
Staff Manager   15 Jul 86

Distribution

All departmental managers & supervisors
All staff notice boards

9   Essential bric-a-brac

This final chapter offers sample bits and pieces on a wide miscellany of writing tasks which, thanks to Sod's Law, often spoil Bertie Manager's day. Here's hoping they'll be of help.

Notices of meetings

Formal notice of an annual general meeting – Sample   (118)

UPPERS AND DOWNERS PHARMACEUTICALS LTD

Notice is hereby given that the Seventh Annual General Meeting of the Shareholders of Uppers and Downers Pharmaceuticals Limited will be held at the Bent Horseshoe Hotel, Lerwick, Shetland Islands, on the 15th day of August 1986 at 10.00 a.m. for the purpose of considering the Directors' Report and Statement of Accounts for the year ending 31st March 1986; of declaring a dividend; of electing Directors and appointing Auditors; of transacting any other general business of the Company requiring transaction. A member entitled to attend and vote is entitled to appoint a proxy to vote in his stead; such proxy need not be a member of the Company.

Dated this 17th day of July 1986
By order of the Board

Charles Uppingham
Secretary

Notice of a club annual general meeting – Sample   (119)

THE BARFORD ST GILES GUILD OF GENTLEWOMEN

'Broody Perch'
Cow Lane
Barford St Giles
Cambs PE26 6QW   11 July 1986

Dear Miss Abbots-Linchley

The Annual General Meeting of the Guild will take place at the Village Hall, Barford St Giles, on 2 August 1986 at 7.00 p.m. I do hope that you will be able to attend.

A copy of the agenda for this meeting is enclosed.

Yours sincerely

Dorothea Snitch
Secretary

Notice of a Directors' meeting – Sample (120)

THE EAST STRATTON CAVIAR COMPANY LTD
The Hatchery, East Stratton, Hants
(Tel: 0487 912862)

SBC/34/2/1   21 August 1986

Lt Cdr H J Snodgrass, RN (Rtd)
c/o The Admiral Benbow Inn
Clopton Magnus
Beds

Dear Sir

The next meeting of the Board of Directors of The East
Stratton Caviar Company Limited will take place on 4
September 1986 at 11.00 a.m. in the Board Room.

Yours faithfully

S B Carruthers
Company Secretary

Notice of a club meeting – Sample (121)

CRINGE CRICKET CLUB

NOTICE OF MEETING

A meeting of the Cringe Cricket Club Bar and Social
Amenities Committee will be held at 8.00 p.m. on 1
July 1986 in the Anteroom to the Club Bar.

I V A Slurp
Hon Secretary

Agenda for meetings

Agenda – Table of contents   (122)

Election of chairperson (if required)
Reading of notice of meeting by secretary (if required)
Reading of minutes of last meeting by secretary
Points arising from minutes as read
Reading by secretary of any correspondence received since
   the last meeting
Chairperson's opening comments
Any business adjourned from the last meeting
Financial matters (report by the treasurer, approval of
   expenditure, circulation of accounts, etc.)
Reports by sub-committees, working parties, etc.
Election of officers (if required)
Motions to be placed before the meeting
Date of next meeting
Any other points of minor business

Agenda – Sample   (123)

THE EAST STRATTON CAVIAR CO LTD

Directors' Meeting to be held on 4 September 1986 at 11.00 a.m. in the Board Room

AGENDA

1   **Apologies for absence.**
2   **Minutes of the meeting held on 1 August 1986 (copies circulated).**
3   **Matters arising from the minutes**
    (a)   Minute No. 8 should be amended as follows: for '1,000 tons of lumpfish caviar' read '10 ozs of lumpfish caviar';
    (b)   Minute No. 11 – New Products. The Chairman

has decided that he can no longer support the Board's decision to market edible frog spawn under the trade name of British Bullfrog Caviar-Type Appetizer.

4 **Correspondence**
A letter has been received from the Comptroller of the Privy Purse concerning the sturgeon recently purchased by the Company from the Thames Angling Club.

5 **Motion**
That a committee be formed to consider the viability of cross-breeding the Caspian Sea Sturgeon (Acipenser) with the Common Flounder for the eventual production of small-bore caviar.
Proposed: Major Hopcliffe-Pugh
Seconded: Miss Titmarsh

6 Date of next meeting.

7 Any other business.

Minutes of meetings

Compiling minutes – Checklist (124)

1 During the meeting concerned, remember to make a list of those present and those from whom apologies for absence have been received.

2 Notes made during the meeting should be as short as possible. They should reflect an impartial and balanced summary of what has transpired; and, where possible, the names of speakers should be included (normally, not for inclusion within the minutes, but merely for use as a memory-prodder when compiling them).

3 Ensure that minute items are related to, and presented in the same order as agenda items.

4 Itemize matters raised under Any Other Business.

Minutes of a meeting – Sample   (125)

THE EAST STRATTON CAVIAR CO LTD

<u>Minutes of the Directors' Meeting held on</u>
<u>4 September 1986</u>
<u>at 11.00 a.m. in</u>
<u>the Board Room</u>

Present: The Hon Montague Pratt (Chairman)
Major G M Hopcliffe-Pugh, RA (Rtd)
Mr S T Isinglass
Lt Cdr H J Snodgrass, RN (Rtd)
Miss J D Titmarsh

1   <u>Apologies for absence</u> Apologies for absence were received from Mr B A Hinckley and Mrs J Lewis.

2   <u>Minutes</u> The minutes of the meeting of 1 August 1986 were taken as read. The following amendment was made:

   Minute No. 8   The reference to '1,000 tons of lumpfish caviar' was incorrect and was changed to read '10 ozs of lumpfish caviar'.

   The minutes were then approved as a correct record and signed by the Chairman.

3   <u>Matters arising</u>

   Minute No. 11   The Chairman informed the meeting that, following the most careful consideration of all the factors involved, he could no longer associate himself with the Board's decision to market edible frog spawn under the trade name of British Bullfrog Caviar-Type Appetizer. All present signified their deep regret.

4 <u>Correspondence</u> The Secretary read out the contents of a letter received from the Comptroller of HM Privy Purse concerning the sturgeon recently purchased by the Company from the Thames Angling Club. It was unanimously resolved

> THAT the Chairman writes a letter of apology to the Comptroller of HM Privy Purse in regard to the Company's inadvertent acquisition of Royal property, and that the 1.5 oz jar of caviar derived from HM the Queen's sturgeon be presented to Her Majesty as a token of the Company's heartfelt loyalty and regret over the unfortunate incident.

5 <u>Product research</u> The meeting considered a proposal from Major Hopcliffe-Pugh, seconded by Miss Titmarsh, that a committee be formed to consider the viability of cross-breeding the Caspian Sea Sturgeon (Acipenser) with the Common Sea Flounder for the eventual production of small-bore caviar. It was unanimously resolved

> THAT Major Hopcliffe-Pugh and Miss Titmarsh comprise the said committee and that the committee reports on its findings at the next meeting.

6 <u>Date of next meeting</u> It was agreed that the next meeting will be held on 7 October 1986 at 11.00 a.m., in the Board Room.

7 There being no further business, the Chairman declared the meeting closed at 12.20 p.m.

Invitations
Formal invitation – Sample 1 (126)

The Managing Director
[*and Managers*] [*and Management Team*]
[*and Executive Team*]
of The Crushit Truss Company Limited
request the pleasure of the company of

....

at the launch of the Armorclad Super-Truss range
at Stayput House, Friern Road, Pitsea, Essex
on Friday, 4th July 1986, at 7 p.m.

The Sales Director
The Crushit Truss Co Ltd
Stayput House
Pitsea   RSVP
Essex   by 27 June 1986

Formal invitation – Sample 2 (127)

Mr and Mrs Ronald Plackett
request the pleasure of the company of
....
at [*a*] [*the*] ....
at ....
on ....
[*and afterwards at*]
[....]

12 Mudbank Flats
Pockley,   Essex   RSVP

Acceptance of formal invitation – Sample 1   (128)

Mr [*and Mrs*] Martin Throgmorton
thanks [*thank*] the Managing Director
of the Crushit Truss Company Limited
for his invitation to attend the launch
of the Armorclad Super-Truss range
on 4th July 1986, at which he [*they*]
will be happy to be present

23 The Brink
Churchend
Foulness Island
Essex   24 June 1986

Acceptance of formal invitation – Sample 2   (129)

Mr [*and Mrs*] Martin Throgmorton
thanks [*thank*] Mr and Mrs Ronald Plackett
for their kind invitation to
....
at ....
on ....
and has [*have*] much pleasure in accepting

23 The Brink
Churchend
Foulness Island
Essex   6 August 1986

Refusal of formal invitation – Sample 1   (130)

Mr [*and Mrs*] Martin Throgmorton
thanks [*thank*] the Managing Director
of the Crushit Truss Company Limited
for his invitation to attend the launch
of the Armorclad Super-Truss range
on 4th July 1986
but regrets [*regret*] that owing to a prior
commitment he [*they*] will not be able to be present

23 The Brink
Churchend
Foulness Island
Essex   24 June 1986

Refusal of formal invitation – Sample 2   (131)

Mr [*and Mrs*] Martin Throgmorton
thanks [*thank*] Mr and Mrs Ronald Plackett
for their kind invitation to
....
at ....
on ....
but regrets [*regret*] that owing to a prior
engagement he is [*they are*] unable to accept

23 The Brink
Churchend
Foulness Island
Essex   24 June 1986

Informal invitation – Sample   (132)

THE CRUSHIT TRUSS COMPANY LIMITED
Stayput House Pitsea Essex

Directors:
A M Amazon
C K Atlas
I M A Trojan

Telephone: 0897 342156
Cables: Titefit London

AMA/43/23/1   **17 July 1986**

Mr C A Seagram
17 Sewage Works Road
Pitsea
Essex PT33 7GG

Dear Mr Seagram

We are very pleased to announce that we have just completed our move into ultra-modern, custom-built premises at the above address.

To mark this significant event in the history of our Company, we are holding a Buffet Reception for our regular customers on Thursday, 31 July at 7.30 p.m. and would much value the pleasure of your company.

In order that we can finalize our arrangements, perhaps you would kindly let me know by 25 July if, as is our hope, you will be able to attend.

Yours sincerely

C K Atlas
Sales Director

Acceptance of informal invitation – Sample   (133)

Mon Repos
17 Sewage Works Road
Pitsea
Essex PT33 7GG
(Tel: 0897 345662)

C K Atlas Esq   **19 July 1986**
Sales Director
The Crushit Co Ltd
Stayput House
Pitsea
Essex

Dear Mr Atlas

**Thank you for your kind invitation to the Buffet Reception
on 31 July, which I will be happy to attend.**

Yours sincerely

Chas A Seagram

Refusal of informal invitation – Sample   (134)

Mon Repos
17 Sewage Works Road
Pitsea
Essex PT33 7GG
(Tel: 0897 345662)

C K Atlas Esq   **19 July 1986**
Sales Director
The Crushit Co Ltd
Stayput House
Pitsea
Essex

Dear Mr Atlas

Thank you for your kind invitation to the Buffet Reception on 31 July. I much regret that owing to a prior commitment I will not be able to attend.

Yours sincerely

Chas A Seagram

Press releases

Compiling press releases – Checklist (135)

1 Always include details of any embargo (i.e., advance information released to the press on the understanding that it will not be published before a specified date). If there is no such embargo, confirm this with the phrase 'For Immediate Release'.
2 *Format*:
   (*a*) Type on one side of the paper only.
   (*b*) Use double spacing throughout.
   (*c*) Leave wide margins for editing purposes.
   (*d*) Use follow-on catch lines at the foot of each page (i.e., /*this amazing product . . .*).
   (*e*) Finish the release thus:
   – ends –
3 Outline the main gist of the release in the first paragraph. Utilize successive paragraphs for the provision of more detailed information.
4 Ensure that the release is 'tailored' to the publication concerned; i.e., that the overall style is suited to the readership.

5   Check and double-check every word, especially technical data, for accuracy.

6   Always include the name and telephone number of someone who can be contacted for further information.

Press release – Sample   **(136)**

WILLIAM HEINEMANN LTD

PRESS RELEASE   Wm. Heinemann Ltd
                                     10 Upper Grosvenor St
                                     London W1X 9PA
3 October 1986   Tel: 01 493 4141
For immediate release   Telex: 8954961

A NEW BOOK

THE SECRETS OF SUCCESSFUL
BUSINESS LETTERS

Clive Goodworth

This practical, down-to-earth book offers a self-help cure for one of any manager's biggest headaches – how to write good business letters for a multitude of purposes. In addition to offering sound, sensible advice on effective business writing, Clive Goodworth provides a veritable arsenal of ready-made placatory letters, pay-up-or-else letters, selling letters, selection and recruitment letters, letters of praise and the wielding of the big stick – and backs them all up with invaluable tips on dos and don'ts.

The contents include: Placatory writing – apologies for poor service, delays, failures to supply, faulty goods, replies to ill-founded complaints, pleasant but firm rejection of complaints; Pay up or else – initial reminders to settle and successive reminders; Flogging one's wares; Technical writing; Selection and Recruitment writing; Laudatory letters – promotion, pay increases, etc.; Disciplinary writing – formal warnings, dismissals, orders, rules and instructions; Miscellany of letters including notices to attend meetings, agenda, minutes of meetings, formal/informal invitations, press releases, annual reports, etc.

About the Author

Clive Goodworth has worked as a training adviser in the road transport industry, and as senior personnel executive to an international oil company. In more recent years he was Senior Lecturer in Professional and Management Studies at the Huntingdonshire College. Now much in demand as an accomplished speaker and raconteur, he devotes most of his time to writing. His previous books include *Effective Interviewing for Employment Selection*, *Effective Speaking & Presentation for the Company Executive*, *How to be a Super-Effective Manager*, *How You Can Do More in Less Time*, *Effective Delegation* and *Taking the Strain*.

The Secrets of Successful Business Letters is an indispensable guide for anyone working in business who writes, as well as students on business and office practice courses.

ISBN 0 434 90684 3   138mm/Hardback/£12.95

— ends —

For further information, please contact Edward Cross (Tel: 01 493 4141).

PROFESSIONAL AND TECHNICAL

Annual reports, etc.

Annual reports and other blurbs – Phrase-bank   (137)

. . .advancing trend of your Company's profits. . .

. . .will make a very considerable impact on. . .

. . .I claim no credit for the startling growth. . .

. . .it has been a privilege and a pleasure to work. . .

. . .work with them serving your interests. . .

. . .I have the greatest confidence that the Company is in good hands. . .

. . .it is now our intention to place emphasis on building up this. . .

. . .and in furtherance of this policy. . .

. . .an important development in your Company's. . .

. . .in common with virtually all companies, we experienced a reduction in. . .

. . .the problem is one of balance. . .

. . .this growth contributed to. . .

. . .the achievement of the high performance. . .

. . .which we seek for the longer term. . .

. . .our policy of building up. . .

. . .I warned shareholders last year. . .

. . .which has seen a pause in the growth of our profits. . .

. . .in common with most other UK commercial businesses. . .

. . .as to the present year. . .

. . .the year saw the continuance of our development of. . .

. . .the operating groups are now well placed to. . .

. . .results were also affected by. . .

. . .trading well and better results can be expected. . .

. . .in the current difficult conditions. . .

. . .the strengthening of our overall corporate position in. . .

. . .gives rise to hopes of a bright future. . .

. . .in general, 19... was a difficult year. . .

. . .the year has been one of considerable growth in. . .

. . .the results for the group were affected by. . .

. . .the strong base-level of trading. . .

. . .the storm clouds of depression. . .

. . .the monolith spectre of unemployment. . .

. . .wildly fluctuating investment climate. . .

. . .the damaging effects of a depressed world economy. . .

. . .the unstinted efforts of your management. . .

. . .the eye of the hurricane. . .

. . .pause for reflection and consolidation. . .

. . .surpassed beyond all expectations. . .

. . .demanded retrenchment and a severe curb on. . .

...planning for posterity...
...dedicated and hard-working team...
...some adjustments in personnel were...
...rationalization of our resources...
...the inescapable facts of economic life...
...your Company will weather the storm...
...occluded by the clouds of a depressed market...
...virtually unrestrained and wholly destructive import levels...
...the dividend remains well covered...
...we are discussing arrangements with...
...you will also recall that last year's report...
...the balance sheet has been greatly strengthened by...
...we are not expecting any great advance over 19......
...it would be wildly optimistic for me to...
...developed and produced with optimum efficiency and economy...
...times are always changing...
...and nowhere faster than in the UK industrial field...
...but to ensure as a practical reality the realization that...
...it is with this aim that...
...individuals contributing to a single goal...
...as part of your management's new look at...
...during 19..., there will be launched...
...a challenging and exciting future...
...our people are our most valuable asset...
...despite all this, the loyalty and enthusiasm of our...
...I confidently believe we have rounded the corner...
...with the continued and unstinted support of...
...a turning-point in your Company's fortunes...

. . .a year of challenge, opportunity and achievement. . .
. . .is not a time for pessimism. . .

Obituaries

Stop-press obituary – Sample   **(138)**

OBITUARY

Brian (Chalkie) White

Director/General Manager, Ash Products (Ramsey) Ltd

On the 9th July Mr Brian White, after a brief
illness, died at his home in March.
Brian was 44 years of age and we would extend our
most sincere and deepest sympathy to his family in
this tragic loss which is shared by all of us
at the Ash Group.

As this Journal was already printed when the news
was first known, a full tribute will be printed in the
next issue of Ash News.

Obituary – Sample   **(139)**

OBITUARY

Brian (Chalkie) White

Brian White joined the Ash Group headquarters in 1966 as
an administration supervisor and, from the outset of his
tragically brief career, displayed an enviable flair for
organization and management. His aptitude and enthu-

siasm for the job found early reward in 1969 when he won promotion to the post of administration manager at Ash Products (Oxford) Ltd, where he swiftly gained a reputation as a manager 'par excellence'.

It is difficult to describe Brian's career without resort to superlatives – but, in fact, the evidence speaks for itself. He was appointed Assistant General Manager at Ash Products (Liverpool) Ltd in 1974, and General Manager in 1977. In 1982, Brian was appointed Director/General Manager of Ash Products (Ramsey) Ltd and, as chief executive of this company, once again demonstrated the particular brand of tenacity and zest for the job which so characterized his working life.

Brian's sudden death at the age of 44 was a profound shock to all who knew him and, on behalf of his many friends and colleagues, we extend our most sincere and deepest sympathy to his family in their tragic loss. He will be greatly missed.

Condolences on illness, injury and death

Letter of sympathy to subordinate on wife's illness – Sample   (140)

Dear George

I was very sorry to hear of Mary's illness, and do hope that she will soon be on the way to complete recovery.

Please let me know at once if there is any way in which I can be of help.

Yours sincerely

Mike Saunders

Letter of sympathy to sick subordinate –
Sample   (141)

Dear Gerald

I was very sorry to learn that you had been whipped into hospital, and do hope that by the time this note reaches you, you will be well on the road to complete recovery.

[*Above all else, do not fret about the work-scene – just bide your time and concentrate on getting fit and well!*] Do please let me know if there is any way in which I can be of help, won't you?

With best wishes from us all,

Yours sincerely

Dennis Bachelor

Letter of sympathy to injured person –
Sample   (142)

Dear John

It came as a considerable shock to hear about your unfortunate [*dreadful*] accident – and I do hope that by the time you get this note you will be well on the road to complete recovery [*and I do hope that you will soon be on the mend*].

Right now, the important thing is to concentrate on the business of getting better [– *so, knowing you as I do, please don't start getting yourself into a fret over the work-scene, will you?*].

Remember, if there's any way in which I can be of help, you have only to ask.

With best wishes [*from us all*],

Yours sincerely

Brian Forbes

Letter of sympathy to wife of sick employee – Sample (143)

Dear Mrs Jenkins [*Cynthia*]

We were very sorry to hear of Ron's illness, and hope that [*he will soon be on the mend.*] by the time this note reaches you, he will be well on the road to complete recovery.

This must be a very worrying time for you – please let me know immediately if there is any way in which I can be of help.

With very best wishes,

Yours sincerely

John Brand

Letter of condolence to widow of deceased employee – Sample   (144)

Dear Mrs Bright [*Gladys*]

We were [*I was*] shocked to hear of your tragic loss.

Please be assured that you have our [*my*] deepest sympathy – and do not hesitate to contact me if I can be of the slightest help.

Yours sincerely

Doug Williams

Informal letter of condolence – Sample   (145)

(*Note*   Such a letter should be handwritten, not typed.)

My dear Jim [*Grace*]

The written word seems so futile at a time like this, and yet I do wish you to know how deeply [*Anne and*] I sympathize with you on your tragic loss.

[*Remember, if there is anything I (we) can do, you have only to ask.*]

Yours sincerely [*affectionately*]

Bob [*Hirst*]

Redresses of grievance, etc

Redresses of grievance, etc – Phrase-bank   (146)

. . .as I think [*hope*] you may agree, things have now reached the point. . .

. . .it is with great reluctance that I now make this formal approach. . .

. . .since my professional capabilities have now been called into question. . .

. . .I thus find it necessary to defend my action in this matter. . .

. . .I now find myself in the invidious position of. . .

. . .vital to protect my own interests. . .

. . .it is little short of ludicrous to even suggest that. . .

. . .I must insist that. . .

. . .the fact that .... years' unquestioned performance should culminate in. . .

. . .I find it difficult to understand. . .

. . .in essence, a refusal by .... to [*even attempt to*] appreciate [*understand*] [*cooperate*]. . .

. . .throughout my entire service [*many years of service*] I have never encountered. . .

. . .such [a] flagrant disregard for. . .

. . .I deem it relevant [*pertinent*] to add. . .

. . .come what may, I will not countenance. . .

. . .such rankly unfair (*unwarranted*] treatment. . .

. . .a quietly insidious campaign of. . .

. . .is, without question, the most difficult working relationship I have ever. . .

. . .totally lacking in reason [*or, for that matter, desire to offer any form of co-operation*]. . .

. . .has been blown up out of all proportion. . .

. . .is quite the last straw. . .

. . .despite every effort on my part, has adamantly refused to co-operate. . .

. . .has met with a blank refusal. . .

. . .entirely lacking in merit or foundation in fact. . .

. . .I absolutely refute [*deny*] the allegation[*s*] . . .

. . .this is not merely a point of principle. . .

. . .I can state with absolute conviction that. . .

. . .the facts in this matter speak for themselves. . .

. . .it should be understood that I will take every step open to me to obtain. . .

. . .an equitable conclusion [*decision*] [*outcome*]. . .

. . .the principle of natural justice. . .

. . .has been completely flouted [*ignored*]. . .

. . .in all the circumstances, I must insist. . .

. . .a formal and thorough investigation. . .

. . .an examination of the facts will reveal. . .

. . .[*will*] grossly and adversely affects [*affect*] my position as [*a manager*]. . .

. . .for which I now seek redress. . .

. . .my hope that this matter can be settled without recourse to. . .

. . .my last wish is to be placed in a position where I have no alternative but to consult my solicitor. . .

. . .constitutes [*is tantamount to*] a serious [*flagrant*] breach of contract. . .

. . .drives an effective wedge through the regulations [*my contract of employment*]. . .

. . .is completely contrary to. . .

. . .smacks of rank unfairness and an utter disregard for the basic principles of good management. . .

. . .that a decision is made without further delay. . .

. . .that I now ask for your formal support. . .

. . .it is my hope that this [*further*] approach will. . .

. . .confirm the truth in this matter. . .

. . .obtain a reversal of the earlier decision. . .

. . .thereby achieve [*at least a modicum of*] justice. . .

. . .will bring about a speedy and equitable decision in this unfortunate [*worrying*] matter. . .

. . .will confirm that my action[*s*] was [*were*] fully justified. . .

Resignations

Letter of resignation – Sample 1   (147)

Dear Ghengis [*Mr Khan*]

Kindly accept this letter as formal notice of my intention to quit my employment on 31 August 1986.

[*I should be grateful if you would ensure that my final salary payment includes. . .*]

Yours sincerely

John Doe

Letter of resignation – Sample 2   (148)

Dear Michael [*Mr Crisp*]

It is with much regret that I must ask you to accept this letter as formal notice of my intention to quit my employment with Brown Bros Ltd on 31 August 1986.

I have thoroughly enjoyed my five years with the company, and would like to assure you that my

decision to resign [*has not been taken lightly and*] arises solely from the need to advance my career.

Yours sincerely

Geoffrey Stainton

Letter of resignation – Sample 3   (149)

Dear George [*Mr Spreckley*]

[*Having given much thought to the matter of our recent discussion,*] It [*it*] is with [*profound*] regret that I must [*now*] ask you to accept this letter as formal notice of my intention to quit my employment with Beezeley Ltd on 31 August 1986.

[*I would like to take this opportunity to thank you for your much-valued support over the past five years.*]

Yours sincerely

Arthur Young

A postscript

And that, reader, is yer lot! When your next Red Alert poops off, I hope that you'll find at least a part-solution to your penmanship hiccup within these pages. Here's wishing you bags more strength to your writing elbow. . . .

Appendix 1

Forms of address, etc

Type of communication	Address	Salutation	Complimentary Close
Letter addressed to a company, but not to a named individual within that company	The Lampblack Laundry Ltd Soapsuds Lane Ramsey Cambs PE17 7QT *or* The Lampblack Laundry Ltd Accounts Dept Soapsuds Lane Ramsey Cambs PE17 7QT	Dear Sirs	Yours faithfully J B Polinski Sales Manager *or, if you wish to be really pedantic* Yours faithfully Stokes & Co Ltd J B Polinski Sales Manager

Letter addressed to a certain individual within a company	The Personnel Officer Exotic Fruits Ltd Pineapple House Exeter Road Huntingdon *or* L D Sprocket Esq Personnel Officer Exotic Fruits Ltd etc.	Dear Sir *or* Dear Madam *(But never Dear Sir or Madam)* Dear Mr Sprocket	Yours faithfully F D Golightly General Manager Yours sincerely F D Golightly General Manager
Letter addressed to an individual	L D Sprocket, Esq MBE BSc 13 High Meadow etc. *or* Mr L D Sprocket 13 High Meadow etc.	Dear Sir *Or, informally* Dear Mr Sprocket	Yours faithfully Yours sincerely

Notes

1   *Addressing the ladies*   As indicated above, letters to women, married *or* unmarried, formally open *Dear Madam*. If in any doubt regarding the sex of your correspondent, always use the salutation *Dear Sir*.

2   *Titles, orders & decorations*   If, when writing formally, you wish to include such titbits (and they should be included), then the recognized abbreviations should be added after '*Esq*' in the following order:

Orders – Decorations – University degrees – Professional qualifications – Abbreviations indicating professions.

Appendix 2

Abbreviations – Commercial terms

A/C, a/c	account
ad lib.	(*ad libitum*) to the extent desired
App., app.	appendix
b/d	brought down
b/f	brought forward
B/L	bill of lading
B.S.I.	British Standards Institution
c/d	carried down
c & f	cost and freight
c.i.f.	cost, insurance and freight
C.P.A.	critical path analysis
C.O.D., c.o.d.	cash on delivery
Cr., cr.	credit or creditor
D.C.F.	discounted cash flow
Dr., dr.	debit or debtor
E.D.P.	electronic data processing
e.g.	(*exempli gratia*) for instance
E.M.I.P.	equivalent mean investment period
E & O.E.	errors and omissions excepted
et seq.	(*et sequentia*) and what follows
f.a.a.	free of all average
f.a.s.	free alongside ship
f.o.b.	free on board

f.p.a.	free of particular average
Hon. Sec.	Honorary Secretary (not Honour*able*)
H.P.	hire purchase
ibid.	(*ibidem*) in the same place
i.e.	(*id est*) the same
inst.	(instant) in the present month
i.q.	(*idem quod*) the same as
loc. cit.	(*loco citato*) in the place quoted
log.	logarithm
l.s.	(*locus sigilli*) the place of the seal
M.S.	manuscript
N.B.	(*nota bene*) note well
n.d.	no date
N.P.V.	no par value
ob.	(*obiit*) died
op. cit.	(*opere citato*) in the work stated
p.a.	per annum
p.c.	per cent
P/E	price/earnings ratio
P.E.R.T.	project evaluation review techniques
p.p.	per pro
P.P.C.	(*pour prendre congé*) to take leave
P.P.I.	policy proof of interest
pro tem.	(*pro tempore*) for the time
prox.	(*proximo*) in the next month
R.D.	refer to drawer
R.P.M.	retail price maintenance
R.R.P.	recommended retail price
R.S.V.P.	(*répondez s'il vous plait*) please answer
s.f.	(*sub finem*) towards the end
subst.	substitute
sup.	(*supra*) above
suppl.	supplement
temp.	(*tempore*) in the period of
trs	transpose
ult.	(*ultimó*) in the last month
v.	(*vide*) see, (*versus*) against

viz	(*videlicet*) namely
W.I.P.	work in progress
x-cp	ex-coupon
x.d., x-div.	ex-dividend
x-i.	ex-interest

Appendix 3

Abbreviations – weights and measures

Length

inch(es)	in	millimetre(s)	mm
foot/feet	ft	centimetre(s)	cm
yard(s)	yd(s)	metre(s)	m
mile(s)	mile(s)	kilometre(s)	km

Weight

ounce(s)	oz	gram(s)	g
pound(s)	lb(s)	kilogram(s)	kg
stone	stone	tonne(s)	tonne(s)
hundredweight(s)	cwt		
ton(s)	ton(s)		

Area

square inch(es)	sq in	square centimetre(s)	cm^2
square foot/feet	sq ft	square metre(s)	m^2
square yard(s)	sq yd(s)	hectare(s)	hectare(s)
acre(s)	acre(s)	square kilometre(s)	km^2

Volume

cubic inch(es)	cu in	cubic centimetre(s)	cm^3
cubic foot/feet	cu ft	cubic metre(s)	m^3
cubic yard(s)	cu yd(s)	litre(s)	litre(s)
fluid ounce(s)	fl oz		
pint(s)	pint(s)		
gallon(s)	gall(s)		

Appendix 4

Meetings – Glossary of terms

Adjournment	The continuation of a meeting at a later date. Note: not a postponement, which is the term used when the original meeting as a whole is put back to a later date.
Ad hoc	Commonly misinterpreted as meaning 'casual', *ad hoc* means, in fact, 'for a special purpose' – hence, an *ad hoc* committee is a committee formed for a specific purpose.
Addendum	An amendment that adds words to a motion.
Amendment	A proposal to alter a motion by adding or deleting words. An amendment must be proposed, seconded and put to the meeting for acceptance.
Casting vote	This is an 'additional' vote usually allowed to the Chairperson – often (but inadvisedly) used to convert a stalemate vote into a decision.
Closure	A motion submitted with the usually desperate object of ending an interminable or unwanted discussion.

Co-option	The power given to a committee to allow others, usually those with specialist knowledge or interests, to serve on the body.
Dropped motion	A motion that is abandoned because there is no seconder, or because the meeting wishes it to be dropped.
Ex officio	An *ex officio* member of a committee holds office by virtue of his or her special position in the organization, and without whose attendance the committee would find it difficult or impossible to function.
In attendance	People who are not members of a committee, but who, nevertheless, are required to be present; e.g., the secretary.
In camera	In private, behind closed doors.
Intra vires	Within the power or authority of the body concerned.
Kangaroo closure	The oft-contested right of the Chairperson to hop from one amendment to another, omitting those which, in his or her view, are trivial or time-wasting.
Lie on the table	A topic or document is said to 'lie on the table' when a meeting decides to do damn-all about it.
Nem. con.	A contraction of 'nemine contra-dicente' – meaning no one is in contradiction.
No confidence	A term which refers to the nasty turn of events when a majority vote of the meeting expresses a lack of confidence in, say, the Chairperson – to the salt mines with whoever it is. . . .
Proxy	A member who acts on behalf of

another, or the document that entitles a non-member to attend a meeting and vote on behalf of an absent member.

Quorum	The number of persons required to be present to constitute a valid meeting.
Refer(ence) back	Temporary postponement of a topic while it is referred to some sub-committee or other for further investigation, etc.
Resolution	A motion that has been carried.
Sine die	Adjourned '*sine die*' – postponed for an indefinite period.
Ultra vires	Beyond the power or authority of the body concerned.

Recommended reading list

Gowers, Sir Ernest, *Plain Words*, HMSO 1948.
Hughes, S. J. and Parsons, C. J., *Written Communication for Business Students*, Edward Arnold 1977.
Turner, Barry T., *Effective Technical Writing and Speaking*, Business Books Second edition 1978.
Wright, Peter, *Language at Work*, Heinemann 1973.

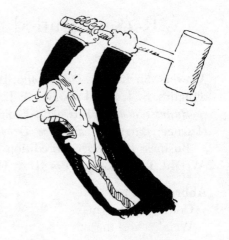

Red alert index

Note Only the main sections of this index are listed in alphabetical order. Subsidiary items are listed (as nearly as possible) in the 'natural order of progression' through the topic concerned.